TRESSELL AND THE LATE KATHLEEN

TRESSELL
AND THE
LATE KATHLEEN

*A biographical memoir
and a message of hope*

D.V. HAINES

Matador
9 Priory Business Park,
Wistow Road, Kibworth Beauchamp,
Leicestershire. LE8 0RX
Tel: 0116 279 2299
Email: books@troubador.co.uk
Web: www.troubador.co.uk/matador
Twitter: @matadorbooks

ISBN 978 1789013 412

British Library Cataloguing in Publication Data.
A catalogue record for this book is available from the British Library.

Printed and bound by CPI Group (UK) Ltd, Croydon, CR0 4YY
Typeset in 11pt Adobe Garamond Pro by Troubador Publishing Ltd, Leicester, UK

Matador is an imprint of Troubador Publishing Ltd

Dedicated, without permission, to all other Tressellians still finding their way to the truth through similar terrors.

CONTENTS

Acknowledgements

Tributes, perhaps, is the better word. But I hesitate to make them.

It might seem as if I am seeking the endorsement of the people who have helped me. My thesis could well be embarrassing to them. Yet the fact remains. I could not even have begun this book without the help of others to confirm dates and other matters. I have therefore left the tributes implicit.

Formal but grateful thanks are due to the Hastings Museum where the Tressell Mural is exhibited. I am also grateful to the Museum for permission to use copyright material from the archives, including the amusing letter by the late former curator Mr J. Manwaring Baines

I have had to omit material where I have been unable to trace the copyright. This omission can be remedied in any future editions if anyone can supply me with details of ownership.

DVH

PART ONE

Looking Behind the Legend

ONE

We call him Tressell, but …

I

… he wasn't. He was Robert, but not Robert Tressell. His real surname was Noonan – and even that wasn't quite real.

Quite a few other things about him – and his daughter Kathleen – were not real either.

In this biographical memoir, I shall be revealing some of the real details about this famously mysterious author which I learnt from Kathleen many years ago. I attempted to reveal some of them in a public WEA lecture in 1980, but I couldn't say too much because of an embarrassing quarrel between Kathleen and Fred.

Fred, of course, was Mr F.C. Ball, an author of high merit himself who had published his copious biography of "Robert Tressell" in 1973. Kathleen had not only begun to detest its title (*One of the Damned*) but Fred himself. He, for his part, had not merely began to detest Kathleen but hate her.

Some four years before he died, Fred phoned me in a rage (a climacteric rage, this being the last time I heard from him). He amazed me by saying of Kathleen (who was living in faraway Bristol): "I'm going to write a secret paper about her. I'll make sure it will be found if I die before she dies, the callous old bitch. She and those bloody aunts of hers left Tressell to die in the workhouse and never lifted a finger."

How did I come to be pig-in-the-middle in such an alarming literary dispute?

It is too long story for me to include every detail, but I can cut a lot of it short by referring you to my sub-title – *a biographical memoir and a message of hope.*

This book is a memoir because of my friendship with both Fred and Kathleen over some twenty years. It is also "a message of hope" because of the values I discovered in exploring the biographical legend which many readers of the great novel (including me) had faithfully believed in. These are not political values, I hasten to add. I am not qualified to comment upon political values except in the vaguest way. I am not even a member of the Labour Party and never have been, despite my admiration for the great novel. Yes, I did vote Labour and I even made donations, and yes – I did once "re-style" the election-literature for the first Labour MP to be elected for Hastings. I'm not claiming this had helped Mr Michael Foster to win his election. He would have won anyway, just as he lost anyway to Miss Rudd when I no longer offered to help with any more "re-styling".

Mr Foster lost, in my view, because the Labour Party will always lose if it loses sight of what we can call Tressellian values. These, I only mildly suggest, are primarily philosophical and artistic values – in short, cultural values.

And they are values which can surely be adopted by any aspiring political party and, indeed, are already to be found (in varying degrees) in all our democratic parties. But politics without culture? Ugh!

Having thus admitted to this much agnosticism, I can only hope that I won't be accused of deriding the Tressell legend as one of Tressell's detractors. (I experienced the flavour of this accusation after I had given the first "Tressell Lecture" in 1980.) To those Tressell admirers who can't or won't question any part of the legend, I can only point out that some of the absurdities in the legend are only too easy for the detractors to pounce upon.

Any present-day attempt to insist upon outdated absurdities, as poor old Fred did (and so many still do), is like handing out ammunition to an enemy.

II

It seems strange to me that I once knew nothing of the man called Robert Tressell – and little of his one and only novel (*The Ragged Trousered Philanthropists).*

The most I had heard of the novel were two passing references, neither of them very enticing.

The very first reference to it was by a chum of mine at our eccentric boarding-school (in Oxfordshire).

"Have you ever heard," he casually asked me, "of a book called The Ragged Trousered Philanthropists?"

"No," I bluntly said, and the matter was pursued no further; for me, this was because the school was run by the Quakers and was more than avid on the subject of alcohol and its worst effects.

Absurdly and lazily, I assumed the book to be about a band of travelling temperance-missionaries.

It was to be years before I was delighting in the title for being deliciously ironic. (I was also later to find that I had not been alone in being misled. Even the book's first publisher, Mr Grant Richards, had initially been misled by the ironic title.)

The second reference was by the manager of a second-hand bookshop, in London and in the City Road. I was working there as an assistant after having joyfully just left school. A big pile of incoming books had been unpacked and the manager was pricing them. He picked up one of the books and said: "Have you ever read this?"

It was a copy of the Pope Abridgement of 1914 (the first edition). I actually handled this now thousand-quid edition but didn't even open it. Although I didn't drink, I immediately felt I'd had enough warning advice to last me a lifetime.

Disparagingly, I tossed the book back on the pile. ("A nice way," said Mr Gutteridge, "to treat a book.")

Without even knowing the book had been written in Hastings, on the South Coast, I set off for that town after a few other adventures. I had no contacts there and was unfamiliar with the locality. My reason for going there was impetuously simple. I had unexpectedly been given the opportunity to rent a mews cottage for ten shillings per week (fifty pence in modern coinage. Far cheaper than London).

I was eager to become a writer. Being young but often stubbornly foolish, I soon went broke.

It was eight years before I actually managed to get anything published – just one smallish book. It only sold about 700 copies, but it did open good doors for me. After 1962, the date of publication, I had plenty of paid-for writing to do, as well as free-lance lecturing. I became neither rich nor famous, I hasten to add, but I did begin to feel more useful to society.

Provided you can earn enough to get by, can any occupation be more rewarding to the spirit than to be paid for what you love doing? Did Tressell himself not find this out? In describing how his main character Frank Owen was asked to decorate a "Moorish" drawing-room, he wrote that Owen "had thought and planned and altered the details of the work repeatedly. The colours for the different parts had been selected and rejected and reselected over and over again. A keen desire to do the work had grown within him."

Is this not a parallel? A Tressellian parallel? In short, a Tressellian value? A cultural value?

It was this and other values which I had yet to discover in the RTP. By 1962, I had still not yet read the book. I was still ignorant of it and the fact that Tressell had lived and worked in Hastings. I didn't know, therefore, that he had lived and worked within a stone's throw of where, in 1962, I was then living. I had married. We had two small children. The mews cottage off Calvert Road was now a nostalgic memory. We now lived on high ground in a house overlooking Hastings Castle and, in the distance, Beachy Head.

Also, I had not yet met Fred Ball.

III

The year 1962, for me, was doubly momentous because, in that same year, my ignorance of Tressell and the RTP was quite magically dispelled.

My ignorance was not unprecedented. Latter-day Tressellians may need to appreciate that Hastings, before 1962, didn't make much of Tressell officially. There was nothing to commemorate him as there is today – no plaques, no roads or passageways named after him and certainly no generous exhibition of his work in the Hastings Museum. Neither the local nor the national press thought him particularly newsworthy. Although there were a lot of Tressell enthusiasts, it is a curious fact that many people even in the Labour Party itself (or sympathetic to it) had somehow remained as ignorant as I. As for being admitted to the halls of English Literature, the RTP was (still is) an outsider.

Although it was to be BBC Television which helped to initiate the later upsurge, it remains a fact that Fred Ball was responsible for making Tressell better known. He did the donkey-work of research. He alone was the one who pioneered the publication of the full text of the RTP in 1955. (One of my reasons for writing this memoir is to plead for greater recognition of this increasingly forgotten fact.) Without Fred Ball, I think it safe to say, the Edwardian appreciation of the Pope Abridgement of 1914 would have been left to peter out. The original manuscript would have been lost. Would there then have been an exhibition in the local museum? Most unlikely. And where would the inspiration have been, which some of us find in the huge, splendidly rough-hewn version of the RTP?

This memoir being a memoir, I make absolutely no apology for making it personal (although, I hope, with decent restraint). But I can give no personal reason why, on a beautiful summer's day in 1962, I left the house and wandered down Wallinger's Walk (past the old abandoned churchyard) and then up Milward Road nearby. In 1962, I have to say, it was a rather shabby road of terraced houses, most of them in flats. (You can see this for yourself when I put my film-shots on the Internet of Kathleen's re-visit.) For now, I only add this: that old post-cards show the road to have been a lot smarter in Tressell's time. The top-flat where he had lived with Kathleen and his sister Adelaide ("Aunt Addie") was by no means a dwelling of the sort depicted in the RTP for Frank Owen.

This stroll was to be my first exit from ignorance. I suddenly came across a newish-looking plaque (a temporary one, I was later told) attached to a house by the street-steps (number 115). There was that odd title – *The Ragged Trousered Philanthropists*! I had never noticed the plaque before and only subsequently learnt, from Fred, that it had been installed in a modest trade-union ceremony earlier in the summer. Apart from a memorial seat on the promenade which I had not yet observed, this was the first public act of homage to Tressell in Hastings. (The seat had been emplaced on the same day as the plaque in Milward Road.)

Without really knowing why, I abandoned my walk (I can't recall where I intended to go) and turned and walked in the opposite direction – towards the public library down in the town-centre. I was only vaguely wondering if the library had a copy of the book which I could borrow. I was not even remotely aware of the further looming coincidences. For me, it was coincidence enough (and only a minor one) that I had just learnt that a Robert Tressell had written a previously-mentioned book. And in Hastings.

In 1962, I must tell you, Hastings was still in a run-down

state after the War. Unemployment was high. Poverty, in some areas, was only a shade less grinding than in Tressell's time. But the town-centre, oddly enough, was a lot more elegant than it is today (in the supposedly prosperous year of 2017). Today, I can't walk through the town-centre without being dismayed. In 1962, it was *always* a pleasure to go into the town-centre, and in particular to the quietly stylish road called Claremont (not far from the sea-front).

It housed the then magnificent public library, a Victorian building of pargetted terracotta with an iron-gate entrance. This was the very same entrance used by many famous people over the years, including Tressell himself. In the very early days, they didn't go in to borrow books but to consult them under the eye of the curator-librarian. I later made a recording of this gentleman's assistant who, aged 19, had sight of a certain man "doing lots of writing" and looking at Hansard. This old boy's voice, like the Agfa cine-film of Kathleen, I shall in due course put on the Internet. The point I'm making here is that the library (locally designated "the Brassey") was still a vital regional centre with a big floor-to-ceiling reference-library.

And my wife was in charge of it, at various future times holding the office of "Borough Reference Librarian" and "Local-Studies Librarian". She had access to now incredibly valuable literary and historical materials (I have a full list) which (in these supposedly better times) have now been vitiated. (What a cultural anomaly!)

Naturally, not finding the RTP on the public lending-shelves in the ground floor department, I ambled up the nobly wide stairs to my wife's domain. I was idly hoping for preferential treatment concerning a possible extra copy.

On seeing me from behind her supervisory desk, she smiled at me brightly and said: "Why aren't you working?"

To remain as objective as possible about my wife's rôle in this memoir, I shall henceforth conceal her real name and call her Angela. It's not entirely a fictitious name. In private, I often addressed her as Angela, this being in honour of the bossy heroine of a girls' public-school story (*Angela of the Upper Fifth*). I ask you to forbear, therefore, that I replied to her opening question somewhat huffily on this momentous day.

"Madam Librarian," I said (another of my names for her), "I am merely having a breather. After all, it is a Saturday."

"When some of us," she was quick to say, still smiling brightly, "have to work. Well? What is your enquiry?"

What I had not known, even after several early years of marriage, was that her opening question ("why aren't you working?") was something of a local joke to people who, like Angela, had been born and bred in Hastings. It stems, of course, from the immortal Misery (the bully of a foreman so brilliantly depicted in the RTP).

You will need, if you are not Hastings born and bred, to practice the intonation if you want to enjoy getting it right. It doesn't sound as it looks in print. It has a sort of idiomatic sing-song inflection which is impossible to describe but which is said, as Misery would have said, to anyone having a breather. ("Woy urn chew wurkin?")

Even Shakespeare, although I'm not claiming he had read the RTP, knew of this age-old reproof. In a military context, he makes it the subject of a complaint by Hotspur.

> "But I remember, when the fight was done,
> When I was dry with rage and extreme toil,
> Breathless and faint, leaning upon my sword,
> Came there a certain lord, neat and trimly dressed,
> Fresh as a bridegroom."

Hotspur goes on to complain that this certain lord ("perfumed like a milliner") took pinches of snuff while hectoring Hotspur and company for their boorish tardiness. Although the unfragrant Misery didn't take snuff, his hectoring was of the same lordly essence. Authority can take a breather and even take snuff, but lesser mortals must not. I didn't, of course, make the connection of this textual link with Shakespeare for quite some time.

It was also a measure of my ignorance, speaking domestically, that I didn't know that Angela had anything to do with Tressell. She certainly didn't have the RTP among her books at home. She was not a Tressell enthusiast, nor did she ever become one; for Angela, Tressell was simply one of her routine literary concerns. She had never mentioned him to me.

"Have you ever heard," I therefore stupidly asked, "of a man in ragged trousers called Robert Tressell? I've just seen a plaque in Milward Road. Isn't that the same road where you lived as a child? He wrote a famous book in Hastings, I gather."

"Tolerably famous," she said, still smiling (or rather, I would say, grinning all over her face), and she came out from behind the supervisory desk. "Come with me. I think I'll leave you to Fred …"

She led me across the room to one of the study-tables. Various members of the public were immersed in obedient silence at these tables, and Mr Fred Ball was one of them – except, to me, he looked alarmingly like Mr Gutteridge. This was the manager of that secondhand bookshop in London, run by the Methodists. He was on my conscience because I had repaid his kindness to me by giving in my notice and clearing off. (One of many acts of youthful folly.)

"Excuse me, Mr Ball," she said, "I'd like you to meet my husband. He wants to learn something of Robert Tressell. You won't mind filling him in, will you? But gentlemen, do please keep your voices down."

Angela returned sweetly and aloofly to her desk, leaving me to fend for myself with this Mr Gutteridge lookalike.

He was concentrating on an open volume of the *Hastings & St Leonards Observer* and then frowningly shuffling through the directories which Angela had heaped upon him. He neither got up nor looked up. I sat down opposite him, the tables being designed

11

for paired study. He didn't seem too pleased by the capricious introduction.

Anyone familiar with Fred in his later career might be surprised to know that he looked nothing like the figure he later became. He was to grow his hair almost to shoulder-length at times, and to dress in a bulkily bohemian way; but this appearance was not entirely an "artistic" pose. Although aged 58 in 1962 and a "late developer'" as an author, he had got two books published; one was a critically well-appreciated first novel (*A Breath of Fresh Air*, 1961) which, of course, I hadn't even heard of let alone given it a read. And, of course, he had valiantly written the somewhat surreal early biography of Tressell (*Tressell of Mugsborough*, 1952).

Speaking to me for the first time, he told me of this latter fact in an abrupt and grudging half-whisper (almost impossible to describe).

"I'm the one who wrote *Tressell of Mugsborough*," he said, having suddenly looked up at me.

This not meaning a thing to me at the time, I could only politely say: "Really?"

"Yes," he said, rather more sternly. "Really! Your wife was my very first researcher. She's been very helpful," he added, but in a tone rather hinting that her help had not always been to the good.

Although a lot older, he looked so like Mr Gutteridge I felt not only abashed but intimidated. His hair was so neat and short that he looked fresh from the hairdresser (as Mr Gutteridge always did), and he was wearing an office-type style of suit with collar-and-tie impeccably centred. Again, like Mr Gutteridge, he was quite slim and dapper. The only major dissimilarity was in the voice. Fred's voice could be described (I think fairly) as rugged.

"Sod this for a lark," he said, suddenly standing up and abandoning his studies. "Like to come and have a cup of tea?"

Without waiting for me to reply and leaving all his books sprawlingly open, he promptly walked out of this big reference-room. He didn't look back to see if I were following him: he appeared simply to assume (and he was right) that I would. For someone who, as I later discovered, could be so pitifully nervous before speaking in public, he had just made an astonishingly rude spectacle of himself. As for Angela, he ignored her as he went out; but she, it seemed, could hardly contain her merriment, (some of it, I have to say, being at my expense). I should just add, however, that Fred was not (in my experience of him) an unbridled fount of bad language. "Sod this for a lark" or "sod that for a lark" was pretty much his profane extent.

To my further surprise, he led the way out of Claremont and into the most genteel of tea-rooms in nearby Robertson Street. Fussily sitting down amid respectable old ladies at the one vacant table, he instantly announced his order: "Pot of tea for two."

A waitress hurried to his side as if he were the world's Supreme Leader. "And any cakes, sir?"

"No cakes. Just one pot and two cups. And extra hot water," he called after her (loudly but not rowdily).

I was now subjected to the first Fred Ball harangue. It was, of course, ostensibly about the injustices done to Robert Tressell, but I couldn't escape the feeling, even on this first acquaintance, that Fred's indignation also included the injustices suffered by one Fred Ball. Within less than mere minutes, I was feeling mentally exhausted. In only a few minutes more, I uncharitably decided to avoid meeting this man ever again. The whole harangue could only have gone on for just under twenty minutes, and I can only beg you to imagine how limp I felt by the time the bill was presented. Matters were not improved on finding (this was to be typically Fred) that the invitation had not been free. I was expected to pay, not only for myself but for all of Fred's share as well. (He hadn't quite enough change, he explained, and he didn't want to split a one-pound note.)

Angela's reaction, when she came home from work on that summer afternoon, was a lot more charitable than mine.

"Oh, Fred's all right," she airily said. "He's as safe as a firework so long as you don't light the touch-paper. Personally, I don't know why he has such a chip on his shoulder. But that's Fred. You have a choice. You either laugh or despair."

Angela was an amazingly young-looking woman but a good six years older than I and a lot more sophisticated. (I had actually thought her to be less than my own age when I met her.) This meant that she had long been coping with Fred when I was still a schoolboy.

"He's always a difficult author to help," she said, "because he's so suspicious. But there's no trace of anything like that in his novel. You need to read it, David. First, though, I suggest you read the RTP," and she produced the 1955 edition of the full text.

This was not a library copy but one she had briefly gone to her parents' flat to borrow from her father. He was a quiet, subdued man but with ambitions to become a Liberal councillor. (For him, as for many, the RTP tends to cut across all political parties and can be secretly treasured for its acute observations about the Forty Thieves – still a popular local name for the Town Council.)

I opened the book in a mood of extreme distaste. I could almost describe this mood as being one of anticipatory loathing, but that, I think, would be putting it a little too strongly.

IV

Like the blissful memory of the first kiss by a childhood sweetheart, my only memory is of my change of feeling when I first read the RTP.

Memory of time and place have dissolved into an ecstatic muddle. For me, what remains vivid to this day is how all my feelings about Hastings – to say nothing of life in general – were suddenly and increasingly crystallised in a series of huge revelations.

I suppose I spent some time on our little balcony overlooking the castle and the sea and perhaps I did sit up late at night. (The RTP does tend to have this unputdownable effect on new readers.) I can only say that I had completed my own reading of it by the next day – Sunday evening.

I was, of course, aided by reading a handsomely printed copy and not one of the densely-printed paperbacks in small type. (The latter, I suggest, should only be bought for reference only.)

The length, I'll admit, is formidable, but not for experienced readers of novels. And yes – it is far from being a perfect work of art. It is not a Rembrandt in words or a Beethoven symphony in words. Yet it is of itself a work of art because of its humanity and its effect upon us as readers – if, that is, we are what is often loosely described as normal.

Before going into what was "normal" about Tressell (and everyone else involved), I would like to end this first panegyric by saying how I feel even when I finish re-reading the RTP today.

"As I close this book, love and reverence possess me."

There are no better words, but those are not my words. They were written by the writer George Gissing (1857-1903) and he couldn't have been referring to the RTP. He was writing of a book containing Shakespeare's beautiful play *The Tempest*. However, according to Angela, George Gissing was the inverse heir to Tressell – a useful thesis she had sought in vain to impress upon Fred. Gissing, she had discovered, had actually visited Hastings with his convalescent wife (some years before Tressell's arrival) and, moreover, the library had an almost complete set of his works in reserve-stock. (These, as soon as Angela mentioned them, I was quick to devour. I particularly recommend the short stories.) For me, therefore, Gissing's words are appropriate. It is love and it is reverence that most Tressellians come to feel for the RTP.

And not only for the RTP.

A love for Tressell himself, it is no exaggeration to say, tends to possess many readers. An idealised image begins to form. The love can be so sensitive that any "rival" image can arouse something

15

very like jealousy. I was not, myself, immune from forming such an image. Although I kept it to myself (especially from Fred), I soon began to see Tressell in the shape of the writer Bill Naughton. He was the father of the chum at school, the chum who had first mentioned the RTP. Like many after–school friendships, this one with the son petered out (and consequently my acquaintance with Mr Naughton), but, as the first writer I had ever met, Mr Naughton had made a lasting and profound impression upon me. He was certainly a suitable candidate for the accolade I secretly bestowed upon him. He was Irish and he had suffered much in early life. But perhaps the greatest similarity to Tressell was his description of himself as a hot-tempered pacifist. That, in brief, is how I pictured Tressell and in many ways still do. (Yet, oddly, Mr Naughton never himself mentioned the RTP when I knew him.)

If I may leap-frog forward to 1974, I did venture to mention Bill Naughton to Fred (with a view to discussing the mutual characteristics) and I got short shrift. Bill Naughton had won the Italia Prize and Fred just missed it. I don't say this accounted for the dismissive snort which ensued, but it was getting obvious that Fred saw Tressell only as an ideal image of Fred. ("Bill Naughton? Haven't seen him for years," implying further contact pointless.)

Leap-frogging back to 1962, I must state that Angela brought me a copy of *Tressell of Mugsborough* to help me to avoid upsetting Fred. She had nothing but good-humoured scorn for this book. ("Fred calls it a biography, but it's far too thin to be a real biography. He wouldn't listen to anything I suggested to give it more weight. Too thin!")

Mr Frank Swinnerton, still a well-known literary-critic in the fifties, was inspired by this "thin" biography to write an elegant booklet *The Adventures of a Manuscript*, 1956). He wrote in a very kindly way of Fred's biography but Fred, being Fred, took offence at Mr Swinnerton's passing reference to "bias". One day, grumpily, Fred suddenly thrusted upon me the booklet saying: "You can keep this, young David. I've no need of it." More about

Mr Swinnerton's details later. At this point, I only wish to refer to one particular obsession which seemed to be afflicting Fred. It was his ridiculous fear of being sued for libel. The biography even included the sour comment that he didn't wish to spend the rest of his life "staring across Dartmoor."

There was no likelihood of Fred being sued for libel – any more than there was for Tressell, to whom he imputed this same fear. I was to check on this issue of libel with two local solicitors and two separate barristers. All agreed the issue was "negated" by the fact that no libel was ever feared by the RTP's first publisher. But, for Fred, the obsession was so acute that it affected the way he wrote his own otherwise evocative first novel (*A Breath of Fresh Air*). Although Angela had told me there was no sign of Fred's chip on the shoulder having infected this novel, it was she who risked suggesting to him that he would have sold a lot more copies if he had "localised" the story with a lot more exactitude. (The story is set in a vaguely anonymous area of his childhood just outside Hastings.) He rounded on her with quite a snarl, repeating his comment from *Tressell of Mugsborough*. ("I don't want to spend the rest of my life staring across Dartmoor!")

She shrugged this off in her usual amused way but said to me, on the way home: "I'm beginning to think our Fred could be described as paranoid, don't you?"

I disagreed. Apart from not being medically qualified to diagnose such a condition, and I may be wrong, I would say that Fred had too much integrity to be labelled paranoid. I have met several people for whom even that amateur diagnosis is justified. All had been pathological liars. Surely that's a leading sign? Fred, as far as I could tell, never faked his research. As Angela herself was to say of Fred's later biography, he lovingly dissected every red-herring with tedious honesty. I give just one example. Certain enthusiasts were very keen to depict Tressell as "fighting against the British" both in the Boer War and in the IRA in Ireland. It may or may not have disappointed Fred to say so, but he said he could find no real evidence and that was that. The only aspersion we can really cast upon Fred is upon the nature of his interpretations. But they were, unfortunately, rather important interpretations … and they were to incense Kathleen.

But did she have any right to be incensed?

This was to be the terribly embarrassing question which, in 1967, was to hit me like an unknown object from outer space. For Fred, however, the question was a deeply personal insult and a lasting injury.

By 1967, you need to understand, all we members of our little clique of local writers had become somewhat cosy. I don't know if the literary atmosphere of those times will ever return now that book-publishing has become so blandly impersonal – and with so many "literary" magazines having gone defunct. Perhaps that time is best described as the fag-end of a genuinely literary era. It had endured from the occasion when Tressell's novel was first published in 1914. We should all be thankful, I hasten to add, that publishing is now becoming a more "democratic" profession. Would that it had been so in Tressell's day! But there can be no doubt that the glamour of seeing one's work in print has faded with the advent of the computer.

Also gone, alas, is the undoubted glamour of the aspiring author actually meeting his or her publisher face to face – just as Tressell's daughter, representing her late father, met Mr Richards in his office at 7 Carlton Street, off Regent Street, in 1913.

It was in that office in that fashionable part of London that Kathleen sold the manuscript. She was not dressed as the drab servant-girl of legend but in clothes bought for the occasion from Harrods. (Her kindly employers paid for them. She was employed as a nursery-governess but treated as one of the family.) It was also in this office that certain "publicity" details were concocted by the publisher, Mr Grant Richards. These, so many years later, were to lead to Fred's final phone-call of denunciation.

That phone-call, as you can already judge, was anguished

enough, but I will now quote an earlier one made to me on Tuesday, June 6, 1967. I don't know if he rang any other members of our complacent clique (most of them were Tressell admirers), but here I can only give my own response to the biggest piece of deceit in the legend which had now blown up in Fred's face.

For the benefit of the uninitiated, I must just explain that legend had it that Kathleen and her daughter Joan were dead and gone by 1918. Both had perished, in Canada, in a motor-car accident. No one, including the publisher, had any further news of them, despite the huge sales of the famous book. (For further details, you will need to consult the biography *One of the Damned*.)

At first, Fred spoke on the phone in a bewildered and subdued tone about this "return from the dead" (as he was later to call it in the new biography).

"It's in *The Times*. My brother rang me yesterday to tell me. Tressell's daughter is still alive. She's just been discovered by a reporter. She's been back in England for ages – living in bloody Gloucestershire."

"But Fred," I said, "this is wonderful news!"

"She's never been in touch after all this time," he said, his voice beginning to tremble. "It's bloody peculiar."

Not at that time knowing of his deeper reasons for feeling so wounded, I gaily said: "You can now check for all sorts of missing details. It will give weight to the details you've already got."

"But I've damn well nearly finished the new biography! This could mean having to revise the whole bloody structure. Years and years of work!"

"Surely," I facetiously said, "you must be pleased to know she wasn't killed after all?"

"Only if she's genuine," he said, growling shall we say like a Canadian bear. "I'm inclined to think she could be a fake. It won't be the first time I've had to put up with fakes and liars. Liars! D'you hear me? Liars!"

"All you need to do," I said, belatedly realising that he needed consolation; "is to tack on a few extra pages to those you've already written."

"Is that what your wife is saying?" He was now becoming belligerent, her criticism of the former biography as "too thin" arising as an old grievance.

"I very much doubt," I made haste to say, "that she's heard anything about this news."

Quite savagely: "They still have the bloody Times in the bloody library, don't they?"

"That doesn't mean she's necessarily seen or even heard what it says. Shall I get her to ring you when she gets back? She's away at a conference."

"I'll deal with this crisis myself, thank you very much. I'll damn well go to bloody Gloucestershire in person," and he rang off leaving me to fear he might have a stroke. (I had seen him go puce with rage over far less a circumstance.)

In *One of the Damned* published six years later, Fred records that he and his wife Jacquie were received "very cordially" in bloody Gloucestershire. Gallantly, he doesn't mention his real feelings; but I believe resentment with Mr Richards and others were the seeds of future discord with Kathleen. Hence that last amazing phone-call (already quoted). With hindsight, I think his resentment understandable and even, in some respects, fully justifiable.

He had been deceived by Mr Richards. Before dying bankrupt in Monte Carlo in 1948, Mr Richards had known that Kathleen and her daughter were still alive and well in Canada. Yet he withheld this from Fred, in London, when he and Fred were discussing both Tressell and the manuscript. Even Mr Swinnerton, in writing his booklet *The Adventures of a Manuscript*, must have known the truth but withheld it. He had been a bosom-buddy of the suave Mr Richards. He had even been mysteriously able to borrow the alternative photograph of Tressell (the one without the famous black Homburg or Prussian trilby as it's sometimes called). This photograph was taken by Louise Osbourne, the paid companion to one of the bloody aunts in Hastings. Fred didn't seem to like this photograph and wouldn't use it for his book, but it was given to me in 1970 and it's the one I like best (hence this book's cover).

Why the deception? What was it that couldn't be revealed to the likes of Fred Ball?

The answer is simple, but perhaps needs to be explained to more modern readers of the RTP. In Western society today, matters of illegitimacy, adultery and divorce are no longer unmentionable. Even in my own lifetime, to say nothing of Fred's and Kathleen's, illegitimacy was so shameful that it could, if detected, earn you the sack. The idea that bastards can't enter the kingdom of heaven is still disgustingly strong enough to be enshrined as a term of abuse, but, on the whole, even bigamy is now dealt with leniently and the children not blamed.

Kathleen was not illegitimate herself. Fred had bluntly checked this possible secret. He said: "I have to ask you this. Are you also illegitimate like your father?" She did, however, desert her husband who re-married without having divorced her. In the eyes of some moralists of her own day, she could have been held to blame for his bigamy, but, by 1967, she surely can't be blamed for choosing to be taciturn. (It was Joan, her daughter, who in 1980 innocently told me of this particular family skeleton.)

Kathleen was a lot tougher, mentally speaking, than people like Mr Grant Richards and Mr Swinnerton and a Miss Jessie Pope seemed to be aware of. With the convenience of historic hindsight years later and after reading Fred's new biography, I realised that all those people had mostly been trying to protect the delicate Kathleen from intrusion. It was Angela, of course, who prompted this realisation.

"Fred," she said to me, after having read the new biography herself, "has always gone at things like a bull at a gate. He will never twig why those people wanted to shield her privacy. She only had to put on her sweetie-sweet voice and she had them all eating out of her hand. She had the same effect on me, at first. But not for long. She's a far darker horse than you and Fred realise. And tougher."

Needing here to speak more about myself for a moment (but more modestly, I hope, than I might speak of Angela), I want to tell you that I was thrilled to the marrow at meeting Kathleen.

It wasn't entirely because she was Tressell's long-lost daughter. I was additionally thrilled because I knew, far quicker than Angela would have given me credit for, that she had a talent for acting.

That's right – acting.

I had no immediate evidence of this talent except, perhaps, a friendly suspicion that she was using her talent to conceal her real-life feelings. She was 76 in 1968. To me, at the time, this was very old, but, now that I'm well past that age myself and still fairly spry, I am even more able to recognise why Angela had been so right. Having now met more than several elderly actresses, as well as a fair amount of "old" ladies – I know that Kathleen – like so many "old" ladies – had a lot up her sleeve in 1968.

Fred, to Angela's witty scorn, was not keen on sharing his knowledge of his research until his new biography was published. He behaved rather like a fictitious private-eye on a case or, as Angela put it, like a child in a nursery-school sitting in a corner and hoarding all his toys. However, since it's possible that you may have read Fred's new biography of 1973, I think I should reveal at this point that Kathleen had told the bluntly enquiring Fred of some of her quarrels with her father. One quarrel was so severe that it caused Kathleen to do a runner. This had scared her father stiff in the way only parents can understand; but, Fred, although a parent, was obtuse about it. She pretended that she couldn't remember what the quarrel was about, but, in a highly private interview with me in 1980, she told me the interesting reason for the quarrel.

"He refused to let me join the amateur dramatic society," she quietly and sadly told me. "I still think him wrong to have forbidden me. But of course I gave in after he brought me home. I loved him so much, you see."

I'm mentioning this quarrel here because it should give you, in advance, a bit of background for the occasion when I made a tape-recording of Kathleen's first words to the Hastings public.

This performance (I do think it fair to call it that) was at a presentation in December, 1968, in the enormous Railway Staff-Association Club.

This building was, and still is, in the forecourt of the St Leonards railway-station where, in August of 1910, Kathleen had waved goodbye to her father. She was never to see him again.

This was his ill-fated trip to Liverpool. He had asked her to buy the ticket for him and to be brave about it. But she pretended to Fred that she was frightened of the man in the ticket-office, thus obliging her father to get the ticket himself. (She had hoped to delay his trip but only succeeded in making him cross.) Fred, of course, believed Tressell to be starving at this time and already dying.

"He had never been in better health," Kathleen was to stubbornly write in the margin of Fred's biography when it came out. But Fred was never to believe her version of events. Although a man of integrity, he was to remain biased in favour of the legend throughout his whole relationship with her.

I, of course, knew nothing as yet of Kathleen's version of the truth. I fully believed in the legend, which, today, is still being repeated. I was merely a member of Fred's contingent when, with Kathleen, we all set off (partly in Fred's car and partly by hired car) to the Railway Club.

We set off from Fred's council-flat on the other side of Hastings. Kathleen was very quiet and self-absorbed but in no way nervous. Fred was the one who was nervous, dreading the possibility that he might be pressed into giving a speech himself. ("Sod that for a lark," he muttered to me.) He was otherwise in what might be called a self-enforced jocular mood. Joan, Tressell's granddaughter

23

and Reg Johnson (her thoughtfully well-behaved husband) were in the same car, but my memory of this exciting trip is very mixed. We were all packed in like sardines. Angela was with Jacquie, I suppose, in the other car but I really can't be sure. There was much jokery and I've no idea where "the Tressells" had their "digs" (as Kathleen called them).

Outwardly, despite the terrible events in America (assassination, police-riots and a strong possibility of world-war three) we were all as joyful as theatre-goers to a fashionable play in London's West-end.

Kathleen, though, as I have said, was quiet.

Very, very quiet but with a self-possessed half-smile on her face – as one would expect, perhaps, on the face of a bit of an old trouper, who, in her time, had travelled far and wide in Canada.

She had even lived in Jamaica, for heaven's sake!

Who could but fail to be bowled over?

TWO

Sold for a Mess of Pottage

I

Before this public appearance in the town where her father had lived and worked, Kathleen had already turned in quite a neat little performance. It was for the benefit of *The Times* reporter who had called upon her to write up his scoop.

"I sold the book for a mess of pottage," she told him, and went on to say: "I don't think there's anything I can do about the book now. I don't want to be rich but I would like to be able to buy some new curtains and I would have liked to have seen the play on television. I wonder if they got the casting right? After all, I knew the people my father had put into the book."

All Fred was to say of this previous little performance (in his biography six years later) was that her remark about the curtains was typical of "the sardonic touch of humour" which Kathleen had "inherited from her father."

I'm afraid I can't agree with Fred's word "sardonic." There was never anything mockingly cynical about Kathleen. Her act (if I may call it that) was always one of titteringly naïve innocence if, that is, she was in a good mood.

Although I didn't know it in 1968 (any more than anyone

25

else), she was using this act to hide her crushing sense of guilt. It was to be upwards of thirteen more years before she was to take me more fully into her confidence. It was then that she revealed her incredibly strong will and her passionate nature. In 1968, self-tormentingly, she believed herself to be the one mainly responsible for her father's inexplicable death and burial. This, basically, was her secret reason for "not making herself known" until persuaded to do so by her son-in-law Reginald Johnson.

It was a well-calculated move after a lot of disinclination on Kathleen's part. It was Mr Johnson who wrote the carefully composed letter to the Editor of *The Times*. Kathleen then had to go into her act as best she could; and you will notice, if you are interested in such things, her revealing reference to matters theatrical – as in the word "casting." (This was but one example of her old-trouper vocabulary.)

She had only been able to take this public step by heaping a good deal of the blame upon her aunt and the rest of the family. She was, when I met her, unscrupulously ignoring the grief they too had suffered and was recall, later, even having accused her aunt of stealing her dead father's post-office money! Fred, I regret to say, did nothing to relieve her guilt or to understand it. He wasn't a bigot, but he was very biased (and there is a difference). To Fred, although he sometimes struggled against the feeling, this was a family who had virtually murdered his alter ego. His rage was like an old smouldering bonfire at the end of a long and deserted garden. I should have known it would burst into flames eventually. With Kathleen pumping away at it with a fire-bellows, this was inevitable.

What have I to say of her 1968 performance at the Railways Club?

Fred didn't want to include the transcript of this recording in his biography, and Kathleen, when I asked if I could keep it for posterity, was equally terse. ("Do what you like with it. It's yours," and she rather oddly added: "What's said is said as Pontius Pilate would say.")

I shall put this recording on the Internet, like others if there's enough interest, but, lest there isn't, I think it should be put into print. It has character-value, if nothing else.

As for the presentation, it was of course due to the sentiment that Tressell's daughter was too hard up to afford a TV-set. As a result of this deprivation, she had been unable to watch the BBC's adaptation of her father's book.

The presentation was made by Mr Leslie Harman, Chairman of the Hastings and District Trades Council. It included not only a television-set on a stand but the licence and even the aerial and a helpful cheque.

For anyone feeling a shade too cynical about this response to the press-reports, may I say that I am also putting it into print because the legend goes that Kathleen "only" received £25 for the book. Not only does she reveal that she received yet another £25 but why, being well fed and not being socially unacceptable, she had been unable to see the play. All I would add, in advance of her performance, was that she did look a bit taken aback by the presentation (although it wasn't entirely unexpected) but rose to the occasion most effectively … as follows.

Whenever a speech is called for, I always feel as though I should say: Friends, Romans, countrymen.

Perhaps on this occasion I can very well say friends, and most astonishing-friends when I consider this: for apart from the very few of you, none of you even know me. It's been very difficult to find words with which to express my very deep appreciation of the kindly thought and the generosity that lay behind the giving of this wonderful present.

You can imagine how frightfully disappointed and frustrated we were when we heard that *The Ragged Trousered Philanthropists* was going to be on television and we couldn't see it. Several of our friends have sets, but none of them could get BBC-2 at that time; and so we just sighed, and tore our hair. Later on, we were able to see it the time it was put on BBC-1 not so very long ago.

Since my son-in-law wrote to *The Times* to say how ironical it was that the last remaining relatives of Robert Tressell couldn't even see the play because they couldn't afford a TV, we had many surprising things happen.

Some people got quite a big shock to find that I was alive and not dead, and then others we have heard from have made several new friends … and corresponded with quite a few others … and have met a few that we have never met before.

At first we had no idea of the great publicity the book had had. You see, I went to Canada, as soon as it was published, practically in 1914. And once, during that time – I think in about 1922 – I had a letter from the publishers to say that the book was doing … had done better than they expected. And they sent me another cheque for £25 – which was what I had received when I first sold all rights.

And then, apart from that, we heard nothing. Neither did I know that the fact of my supposed death in a motor-crash was public property in England.

But when *The Times* didn't publish the letter but instead sent a reporter to see me, it was his article that brought forth the fact that I was still very much alive – so that people wrote to me and said how glad they were to find I wasn't dead after all.

I was rather glad myself. [*laughter*]

Thus since then we have had a very thrilling time, not the least of which is this last thing that has happened to us … and we are, my daughter and I, very very grateful and do thank you very much indeed. [*Sits down.*]

This speech was followed by excited and happy applause. Almost everyone, I think it safe to say, was absolutely bowled over. For me, frankly, this was a heart-thrilling moment. I was in the presence of working-class royalty.

I'm not being satirical here. The older people who formed a delighted and congratulatory circle around Kathleen had endured much unjust suffering. Also, at the same time, they had done battle for human rights. They had helped to pioneer social change. It was as thrilling for me to be in their royal presence as it is for many people to be thrilled in the presence of "real" royalty. I felt both privileged and humble as I lingered in the offing and packed up the tape-recorder.

I'm hoping it won't sound too much like an affectation for me to say so, but my childhood had been what Fred had bluntly called "sheltered." He was right in some respects but not in all. And it was indeed a fact that I, in early childhood, didn't come into contact with the authentic values of the British working-class. These moments after Kathleen's speech were as thrilling as two other occasions when I experienced that actual physical thrill at the nape of my neck. (I feel it even now just to think of these occasions.)

The first occasion (if I may deviate for a moment) was as an older child on a tramcar in London towards the end of the War. Two American "white" soldiers were in the lower "deck" where I was sitting when a "black" American soldier entered at the next stop and sat down nearby. The two "white" soldiers ordered him to get up the stairs to what I suppose they imagined to be the deck for lower-class persons. The "black" soldier was about to obey when the tram-conductress sharply said: "You stay where you are, mate. You're in England now."

And to the two "white" soldiers she said: "You can both scram off me tram if you don't bloody like it," and I'm glad to say they quailed.

The second occasion was much later, in Hastings, when I attended a film-showing of the Bolshoi Ballet at a cinema on the sea-front. (This was once the same music-hall where Tressell and Kathleen used to enjoy quick-fire variety.) It was generally supposed that such a film "wouldn't go down well" with the ignorant low-class persons who attended this often half-deserted cinema.

29

In my experience, this was to be the only provincial cinema where the audience-members (having sat in silence) applauded at the end. The applause was more than respectful and appreciative. It was reverential. I often think today that some entertainers, like many politicians, need to realise that simple-minded people (as they are often called by their betters) are often capable of being simple-mindedly right. (I am quoting here a well-known New York theatre-critic Walter Kerr.) I'll add only that I was as thrilled in that cinema as I was as a child in the tram – and as I was in that club-hall at Kathleen's performance.

But I did hear some mutterings about her "off-mike" conversation. "Bit toffee-nosed, inchee?" and "Why call up that posh paper she's on about?" and even "What's she mean, a dish of porridge?"

And Fred, too, looked uneasy. For him, and many would agree, Kathleen's diction was known as Received English – meaning, to Fred's suspicious ears "received at Court" and therefore a mark of the deepest dye. Not very Canadian. She tended to sound, to Fred and even to me (although I was many years younger than Fred) like those Edwardian "ladies of quality" we had both heard in our youth.

This, for Fred, was yet another terrible blow. He had already suffered a previous terrible blow some twenty years before Kathleen popped up. Again, I am not being satirical.

With the help of the public reference-library in the 1940s (which is when Angela started work as a young girl), Fred thought he had traced a locally surviving relative of the otherwise family-devoid Robert Tressell. And it would be, he was sure, a working-class relative who had suffered Tressell's privations. This would be the case, Fred thought, because Frank Owen in Tressell's book was not only working-class but a self-portrait. Everyone whom Fred had managed to trace as a fellow worker or as a boy-apprentice had said so.

And didn't the title-page itself (of the manuscript sold for a mess of pottage) say so too?

Let us remind ourselves. It said: "THE RAGGED TROUSERED PHILANTHROPISTS," being the story of twelve months in Hell, told by one of the damned, and written down by Robert Tressell."

It did *not* say, "written down by Robert Noonan."

Fred had an explanation for this choice of pseudonym (or pen-name, as many prefer to call it). It was, he always claimed, because the "real" author was afraid of being sued for libel as well as "black-listed" by his employers. I shall return to this claim later in this memoir when I report on Kathleen's unexpected demolition of this claim. For now, I am talking about the reluctant relative (a niece of the self-obscured Robert) who survived as late as 1962 – and in our same town. To poor old Fred's aghast surprise, she was not at all working-class but sod-this-for-a-lark a lady. And one who not only held out on him with information but swore him to secrecy over any revelation of her name.

In searching for the truth about Tressell, Fred couldn't have chosen a tougher assignment. It was a self-imposed assignment, yes, but I shall probably say this more than once: it was an heroic effort. The ensuing biography with its brilliant title *One of the Damned* (which his publishers originally didn't like) is, in Angela's opinion (and mine), one of the great biographies. I'll say why later. For now, I ask sympathy for Fred in discovering this second relative, Kathleen, to be almost as reticent as the bloody niece (Alice). Kathleen did give Fred hell. She was inconsistent, she played hard-to-get, she would agree in one session and then back-track. What's more, she too wasn't working-class (sod it).

Although I became fond of her and actually received a kiss (just below the ear), that was not to be for some twelve more years.

Fred, I regret saying, was just as capable of being "difficult." I think it safe to say that Fred, in the course of his life, succeeded in quarrelling with almost everyone and every organisation with whom he had a relationship. (It goes almost without saying that he was a one-man political party and even a bristling, spiky one-man member of how he saw the working-class.) Many thought him to be a red-hot communist, but he would never have been tolerated in any communist country. Of that I am convinced.

As Angela so often said: "Fred is Fred and that's that. Like it or lump it."

Since Fred had such an influence over the Tressell legend, I suggest we need to understand at least a little about Fred if we are ever to appreciate Tressellian values more fully.

As for understanding more about Kathleen's mess of pottage, I think I need only say that £25 really was a lot of money in 1913. It was still a lot of money after two world wars in 1953 when I arrived in Hastings with just that same amount in the post-office. I thought it a fortune – my capital for setting myself up as a writer.

Fred, of course, knew about these money values and how they compared, but he was often inclined to ambivalence in sounding off about them. Academic economists can give us tables equating these values, but, in reality, they don't easily equate. Too much depends upon the part of the country where people were employed and what they paid, locally, for the items bought. (I can remember buying a bottle of ink for a penny in my childhood. Today in Hastings, I have to pay upwards of nine pounds.) It's about as easy to equate historical money-values as it is to equate human attitudes at their different times in history.

Perhaps the simplest way of keeping a sense of proportion, in evaluating wages in Tressell's time, is to keep the penny-pinching Misery in our sights. His basic wage was £2 per week.

As depicted so penetratingly in the RTP, he was both envied and cursed for doing so well. That sort of sum, from 1900 onwards, was to endure right through World War One with only a slight increase (by today's standards) to the eve of World War Two. The average male wage was then only a few shillings more than £3 in 1938. By 1952 as I remember it, the wage was about

£6 in Hastings and everywhere else (which would have been a handsome sum in Tressell's time).

As for the late sixties in Hastings, this period was, for me, like living in a kaleidoscope. But it wasn't just the money values which were all being shaken up. As you have in a kaleidoscope, there were all sorts of bits and pieces which, in reality, were a chaotic jumble. But, given a shake, the kaleidoscope could make them appear to have meaningful symmetry.

THREE

Another Shake of the Kaleidoscope

I

Some three years elapsed between Kathleen's speech and the rather more notorious episode of the Tressell mural.

I am referring to the truly enormous set of paintings which Tressell himself designed for the chancel of St Andrew's Church (in 1905). I had the distinction (and again I'm not being satirical) of saving just one of the panels from destruction. I was not the one, of course, who restored it. That greater distinction (and I do mean this) belongs to others with far more patience and application.

In talking about the interim between Kathleen's speech and the panel-rescue, I have to say that even that interim was itself rather weird.

Another shake of the kaleidoscope, I would call it.

It began with the fact (which I name as indisputable) that Fred was no slouch as a writer. He was already at work on his second novel (*A Grotto for Miss Maynier*). Also, his prospects for recognition as a radio-dramatist on Radio 3 (the prestigious channel) were excellent. But, for those of us worried about him, he was damaging these prospects. His obsession with Tressell was taking up far too much of his time.

Angela, although she was "only" a reader and not a writer, was the first to urge me to intervene.

"You must use your influence," she said. "He likes you. He listens to you. He even says you might one day blossom into a writer as important as himself."

This exhortation was typical of Angela's dubious sense of humour and she merrily went on: "You will need to be very tactful and walk on eggs. But he has got to be told. You're the one to do it. All this Tressell mania is draining his talent. He can't see he's no longer young. He'll end up in oblivion and obscurity if he goes on like this."

Strangely enough, he was contemplating a play for Radio Three with those very words as the title. (*From Oblivion to Obscurity*, I think it was called; or perhaps it was the other way round. I never heard the play and perhaps it was never performed.) But I had no intention, let me plainly state, of undertaking this hazardous mission. I honestly thought it hopeless and foredoomed.

Two separate matters had convinced me. The first was an ITV series, then coming to an end, about a Victorian detective named Sergeant Cork. To this day, I can still remember how proudly Fred had announced, in his flat, that he had rejected an offer to write for the series. ("Oh, they were really shocked," he said, with a hotly foolish air of satisfaction, "when I got up and walked out. They didn't expect that I can tell you!") This was a really stupid action and showed he had no professionalism as a writer. It wasn't a series I had looked at, but, had he taken it on, as any professional writer would, he might have been able to contribute something special. Also, he would have made a lot more contacts with writers (like Bill Naughton, may I say, who wrote prolifically for TV) and, of course, with producers. But no. Fred was Fred.

On a more personal level, the second matter was destructive to a friendship. A really nice bloke, a Labour councillor whom I can only remember as Ted, had ventured to tell Fred that Tressell was becoming too much of an alter ego. Ted was instantly cast into outer darkness.

"No, Angela," I therefore said, "this is not a good idea. Try it yourself if you like. Count me out."

Angela shrugged impatiently and said: "It's for you lot to deal with Fred, not me or anyone else at the library."

I happily thought I'd staved off the suggestion for good. By "you lot," of course, she was referring to the literary clique I've already mentioned. I held no higher position in this clique, I have to say, than that of a sort of honorary office-boy. I had been suggested for this duty by Angela herself, it being my task to convene the meetings by phoning up the various members. The clique itself, I hasten to say, was not the local Twenty Club started by Rider Haggard and others in the Twenties. That was the sort of dining-club where Her Majesty is toasted ceremoniously. One can hardly imagine Fred or me being elected to such a body, but Angela, who could recite all the Kings and Queens of Great Britain off by heart, was eventually the staunchest of members.

Angela had never attended any of the meetings of the more raffish clique even when held in our own home. Yet it was Angela who, with her marvellous boss, Mrs O'Nions, had instigated the clique by staging an exhibition of its books. They had then suggested that we should ourselves form a club. It was a happy enough idea. We vaguely met in our homes, but, inevitably, the clique petered out after two or three years. But one of our queen-bee lady-novelists (and a great admirer of the RTP) did dare to venture upon the same dangerous ground as the unfortunate Councillor Ted. She was an extremely professional author and died with over forty million in the bank, but, despite her wealth and her fame, she was no snob. Perhaps Angela, who had helped her with her research, had dropped a word in her ear. This lady-novelist whose work Angela described as Enid Blyton for grown-ups (and which I admit I found not to my taste) was far more friendly to Fred than to me. (She had said to me: "You, David, are only a technical writer. Fred and I are creative writers. We are real writers and you are not.")

On the occasion when it was her turn to host the meeting, she would always accompany Fred and me to the front door of her luxury-house. I don't know why we were always the first to be seen out before all the others, but that's how it was: she would even slip her arm through Fred's, never through mine.

One day, after opening the front door and seeing us through, she stayed on the threshold to say: "Fred, Tressell was a real creative writer just like you, but he wasted his talent. I hope you're not going the same way. A creative writer is an artist. That means that you, Fred, should only be obsessed with your art – not politics. Leave politics to the philistines. An artist must stick to his last," and, with that, she gestured us off as if we were a couple of trespassers.

On the way to our respective homes (Fred and I always tended to arrive and depart together from these meetings), Fred indignantly said: "She's the last bloody woman to know what she's talking about. She's not even well-read," and with that condemnation she suffered the fate of Councillor Ted. In other words, Fred would attend no further meetings where she might be present.

For the benefit of Tressell enthusiasts who don't happen to live in Hastings, I hereby expose this lady as being Mrs Catherine Cookson. I do so because, like many of her generation, she suffered the same horrifying anguish as Robert Tressell and his equally illegitimate siblings. Mrs Cookson, as I only later learnt, was even then suffering suicidal depression because of the "stigma" of illegitimacy. This affected her physical health.

Although I couldn't read her books, I am today sadly aware that I could have done a lot more for this lady whom I did genuinely admire despite her salty remarks. But, apart alas from just two moments when I was alone with her, I never felt any sense of togetherness with her. The few words I exchanged held promise of it but little more, and I can still remember how her lips would seem to move in silent speech with mine – which was to happen in exactly the same way with Kathleen when in distress.

There were two matters where I could have been helpful. I could have suggested a meeting between Kathleen and Mrs Cookson. They could have really got down to what bothered them jointly. But the more valuable help, perhaps, could have to suggest where she would find professional help in New York. (I learnt of this better resource too belatedly and will give details later.)

The only practical thing I ever did for Mrs Cookson was to introduce her to the idea of tape-recording speech (my lowly subject as a technical writer). The only "cultural" thing I ever did for her was to lend her my copy of *The Catcher in the Rye* by J.D. Salinger. She was later to write that it "acted like a stringent" upon her, but it remained to some extent true that she wasn't conversant with modern writing. All the New Yorker writers were to her a closed book, yet she tormentingly craved to be recognised as a "literary" writer. She tended to scorn all writing which didn't compare with the impossible purity of the work she secretly aspired to.

I am hoping, perhaps in vain, that this digression into the history of a now defunct 1960's group will emphasise the gravity of illegitimacy in former times. To dismiss it, as so many do today, is to lose what is vital to understanding Tressell. But I admit I had no immediate idea that it was to be Mrs Cookson who inspired the thesis of the Tressell lecture I was destined to deliver much later.

II

My life and the way the Tressell story affected it was to change in a big way after 1964.

To appreciate this change to the full, you will need to understand that I no longer lived in the pleasantly situated house in Castle Hill Road (overlooking the castle of William the Conk). This house, be it noted, was built by the same builder who built the house in nearby Milward Road where Tressell had lived (the house still imagined by some people to have been a slum if not a hovel).

Our lease having ended in 1963/4, we were in a bit of a fix. The rent, for those days, was a bit expensive - £15 per month. It would have been more economic for us to get a mortgage, but, again in those days, self-employed people (such a writers) couldn't be trusted to repay a mortage. Nor could working women of child-bearing age. Angela and I, therefore, took the advice of a Labour Party alderman and applied for one of brand-new council flats on the town's outskirts. We thought it would be temporary, but we stayed for some thirty-seven interesting years.

I, for one, was enchanted with the flat.

For me, it satisfied a very Tressellian value. Our small block of eight flats had what sociologists would call "a good mix" of tenants: A policeman, a self-employed plumber, an all-in wrestler, a Church Army worker, a market-gardener, a teacher, a retired insurance-man and just the one writer (me).

And with another writer, Mr Fred Ball, living a stone's throw away in one of the other blocks!

This was a minor but rather worrying coincidence. I had been striving, I'm ashamed to say, to avoid running into Mr Fred Ball and had been succeeding. Fred in small doses was perfectly all right (as a danger to health). Larger doses would leave me with an oncoming headache. I don't exaggerate. In the days of living on Castle Hill Road, I would catch the public bone-shaker to one of the clique-meetings outside of the town. I would then pretend that I hadn't seen Fred waiting at the same bus-stop (for the village of Pett, for example). I would even contrive to get someone like Cleve Canfield, a writer of popular tough-guy Westerns, to occupy the empty seat beside Fred. Cleve Canfield, in reality, was a dumpy little old lady, but she always seemed able to subdue Fred. Perhaps this was because she was a retired primary-school teacher. I can only tell you that I henceforth respected this sort of teacher and, in fact, I eventually joined a Reader's Group consisting mostly of these teachers and we met for many years. Their knowledge of modern and classical literature was superior to mine and, indeed, many of the writers I had met. Fred, I should add, didn't seem to read much modern literature; but, on the classics, he was so well versed that he could have become a WEA lecturer and thus supplemented his often sparse income. The fact that he didn't was typical of Fred. He seemed to prefer supplementing his income, if he had to, by scrubbing a supermarket floor or reading gas meters. (This was before he retired and got a pension.)

But all these evasion-techniques of mine were now at an end. I was now to be stuck with Fred as a virtual next-door neighbour for many years. Fortunately, he had his wife (younger than himself) and a delightfully young and perky daughter (named Clare, after John Clare the poet). These two people not only made Fred's company more enjoyable; they seemed able in some mysterious way to keep him in balance.

Alas, in spite of these happy influences, the seeds of the rift with the three remnants of the Noonan family were being sown ("the Tressells", as Fred called them). At the core of it was Fred's growing suspicion that Reginald Johnson, the son-in-law, was trying to "cash in" on the Tressell name.

Had that been Reginald's plan, Reginald would surely have been only too keen to promote the popular image of Tressell? The legend of a down-trodden worker "flung into a pauper's grave" was surely more saleable than the truth? Both Reginald and his wife Joan, Kathleen's daughter, were not only keen but anxious to dismantle popular bits of the legend.

Yet I have to admit that Mr Johnson did sometimes strike me as being somewhat manipulative.

And I have to add that Kathleen seemed, herself, to be aware of that. For example, consider just this one sentence in her railway club speech.

"Since my son-in-law wrote the *The Times* to say how ironical it was that the last remaining relatives of Robert Tressell couldn't even see the play *because they couldn't afford a TV*, we had many surprising things happen."

It was during that sentence that I had noticed, despite my euphoria, a little glance from Kathleen and in Reginald's direction. In that split second, it seemed to convey that she disapproved of something she was being obliged to condone. Reginald himself was able to afford a motor-car, or at the very least, able to hire one; but, even more tellingly, it was possible in those days to rent a TV at a low cost if you were too poor to buy a set outright. I discussed my observation with Angela (who had been present at the gift-ceremony).

"Yeah," she drawled, "I noticed. A touch too calculatedly pathetic. I daresay Fred noticed too. All his paranoid antennae were well stuck out that evening and quivering like mad."

"But Reginald does seem," I said, "to want the truth about Tressell to be published. It's a genuine concern of Joan's, and he shares it."

"If you're so sympathetic to little Reginald," was her quick reply, "you should have done more to tone old Fred down. However, as you haven't even tried, all we can do is to wait for the new biography. Let's hope it isn't too paranoid. And at least has the merit of being a little fatter than *Tressell of Mugsborough*."

III

The new biography *One of the Damned* was published some six years later in 1973.

I was immediately conscience-stricken.

Too busy to attend any library book-launch, I had in any case become increasingly estranged from Fred. Yet Angela brought home a copy containing a generous inscription to both of us, as follows: "… with love and grateful thanks for all the encouragement given me in the making of this book. Yours from Fred."

The reason for the estrangement was his behaviour during the rescue of the Tressell panel in 1970, to say nothing of the inevitable confusion during the making of a BBC documentary at the same time. Yes, we were all well-paid by the BBC (I got £40, a lot for the time). I had found that side of the adventure to be often hilarious and always interesting. But, overall, it had been a strain – and with some of the dissension emanating from Kathleen.

She had left Hastings for her home, after I had experienced one or two awkward moments with her; to my amazement, she continued our correspondence in the same innocently skittish way, yet, when she returned for the filming, she was worse than before. It's no exaggeration to say that she was more than similar to Lady Bracknell (in the famous play *The Importance of being Earnest)*.

One day, in our flat, I actually found myself disliking her.

I had gone to no little trouble (with Angela) in establishing her father's method of work. Angela had actually lugged home the very manuals, which she had discovered in the library basement, which Tressell himself must have looked at and taken notes from. (He couldn't have borrowed them because, in those days, the public could only borrow books from shop-libraries. The Hastings public library, endowed by Lord Brassey of Normanhurst was originally for reference only.) These two manuals were *The Practical Decorator and Ornamentist* and *The Manual of Ornament*. I had also had lunch with the Principal of the School of Art to discuss how Tressell would have applied the paint.

These were fascinating volumes and I daresay he took tracings of the many designs which he certainly incorporated into the St Andrews mural.

I also laid out on the table my own photographs of other examples of Tressell's sign-writing.

"Not Dad's work," Kathleen kept saying, hardly bothering to look at the examples properly. "There's nothing of his here. Nothing."

As a schoolgirl, she had attended the very church where her

father had painted the mural; but, since her "return from the dead" she had not set foot anywhere near the place. Yet here she was, being extremely disdainful and even unpleasant.

My problem with her was that I had not yet discovered (as I was to discover later in 1980) that she was harbouring many intricate layers of guilt. Had I known this in 1970 I would have been a lot more sympathetic.

In other words, I would have understood that what I saw as character-faults were, in reality, the symptoms of deep emotional problems.

And Fred's often outrageous behaviour during the mural-rescue were not entirely due to his own very deep emotional problems. Kathleen was actually driving him into what is popularly called a mental breakdown. It is a lasting sorrow that I had not yet understood how or where to point sufferers like them to the good sources of help.

During the mural-rescue, the only useful effect upon Fred was (blessedly!) to have his wife and child on site. We then had what might be called a normal and even a delightful situation. Indeed, I appointed Mr Ron Swaine as site-photographer and commissioned him to photograph all four of us during a pause in our labours. Jacquie Ball, Clare Ball, Fred Ball and I are standing outside the porch of the half-demolished church. It's quite a comic photograph and even Fred is almost smiling. (A copy is with the Hastings Museum.) But you would not believe how Fred behaved in the absence of his wife and child. His own account of the mural-rescue (Chapter Forty in *One of the Damned* is, at best, a struggle to express normality. I don't mean by this that his account is worthless. He does cover some basic facts, but I was never allowed to see his account in proof. Today, I'm just thankful to have that happy photograph).

What, then, is the ultimate Tressellian value which might have helped both Fred and Kathleen to achieve mutual serenity? And indeed for others such as ourselves?

Many more years were to pass before I found this "ultimate" value. Both Kathleen and Fred were estranged before I finished my intellectual trudge (if I may call it that) through the works of Sigmund Freud. It was there, wrongly, that I had thought I would find a guide. In my own defence, I can only say that any lengthy contact with someone like Fred (especially when salvaging a mural) could have anyone reaching for a psychiatrist.

Yes, I did in fact do just that. I actually went to see a psychiatrist for advice on how best to handle Fred. I have to admit it: Fred actually frightened me at certain times during the salvage. He would stand there and rage so fiercely that I frequently found myself wishing that I could somehow banish him. ("I'd sooner see this whole mural destroyed rather than let that bastard have any part of it!") He was referring to Mr Baines, the highly reputable curator of the local museum.

Fred had developed an intense dislike for this gentleman. ("The bastard should have taken care of Tressell's work and made arrangements to have it removed before all this! He just couldn't be bloody bothered!") In the course of these typical tirades, Fred would literally attack a part of the mural and "clean" it to extinction. I physically had to interpose at one stage and remind him that the Museum had put me in charge of the rescue and that the panel I had selected was the paid-for property of the Town. ("I'm not letting Hastings have it! As for that snotty bastard, he ought to be bloody well strung up!") Mr Baines, as far as I could tell, was a fairly harmless person but, of course, rather public-school in his manner. (He still reminds me of a then popular children's entertainer known as Mr Pastry.) He was elderly and on the verge of retirement. He only occasionally visited the site to smile, puff on his pipe and say: "Everything all right? Jolly good …"

I'm casting no aspersions when I say the psychiatrist I went to see was pleasant but unhelpful. ("The man obviously needs tactful handling," was mostly all he could say of Fred.) I left his office with the uncomfortable feeling that he probably thought me a lot more dotty than Fred.

Anyone who might wish to picture the middle-class antics of Mr Baines the Curator will be rewarded if they look for the British film of 1950 entitled *Something in the City*. (Easily found on the Internet.) There they will find the actor known to fame as Mr Pastry. They then might enjoyably understand how someone like Mr Baines could so readily infuriate someone like Fred.

FOUR

Kathleen and the Tressell Mural

I

Having given you as it were a bit of hindsight in advance, may I now leap-frog back to August 19th., 1970?

I need to remove certain false impressions about the part I played, particularly the one that I "discovered" the Tressell Mural. All I discovered was that it was being demolished, along with the church where Tressell had painted it in 1905.

And I cannot say that it was in any way a delightful discovery. In that same month, I had just returned from a mind-changing holiday in Sweden, having been invited over by friends Kurt and Lisbeth Stenquist. I had been "liasing" and working with them under the aegis of the Folk University of Sweden. For a number of years, this had made every summer, for me, an idyllic time in Hastings. As for Sweden itself, it entranced me. It was only because I had obvious obligations to Angela and others that I later had to turn down a very good job-offer. It could have led to "re-locating" – and "re-locating" to nothing less, in my eyes, than paradise.

Angela had come with me on that holiday, but, as I do ungallantly say, she had been as capricious as ever. Normally, this would not be a matter to mention in this memoir, but for the fact that Kathleen had become very intrigued by Angela's life-style – as it is nowadays called. I was in no way such a hit with Kathleen, but it was I alone who had to write the replies to the letters which Kathleen, at first, addressed solely to Angela. Although Angela's mind could be wittily nimble, she was often contentedly silent and "smiling at her own thoughts" (as George Gissing describes one of his heroines).

With all this and other matters to bother me, I was in a rather deflated mood after returning to Hastings and having a morning session with Fred. His complaints about the "difficult" Kathleen caused me to make my excuses and leave his flat with the usual beginning of a headache. I still have no idea why I walked past St Andrew's Church in the mid-afternoon of the date he states in the new biography. I was, as he states, with my two then teenage sons.

I had never been in the church before. I only knew what Fred had told me – namely, that Tressell had designed and had painted a huge mural for the chancel in 1905. (He had checked this with Kathleen.)

Joan's husband had shown me a photograph of this work in all its former glory. I regret having to tell you that it repelled me.

"Let's face it," even Fred himself was later to tell the local *Observer* (in one of his calmer moments and referring to the salvaged panel), "it's no Picasso."

But, as Fred very properly added, it was vital to posterity to preserve something of Tressell's "other" work. With this very same worthy thought in mind, I cautiously entered the church with our two boys after having noticed that just two men were starting to pull it down.

Yes, that's all it was to take to destroy this quite massive steeple-house (as the founders of Quakerism would have called it). Just two men, one with a pick-axe and the other with a sledge-hammer. There was no scaffolding or any other technical or safety-formalities. (The steeple itself, later, was to be felled as simply as if it were a tall tree.)

Fortunately, the pick-axe and sledge-hammer had not yet touched the chancel.

But where was Tressell's huge wall-painting?

No sign of it!

I apologise to anyone offended by the childhood indoctrination which still tends to govern my ideas of taste, but I was relieved to find no similarity to the photograph. To me, the decoration was all the better for having vanished. Every square inch of that chancel, it would seem, had been so richly covered as to create (in the photograph) an atmosphere of gloom and even oppression. The three big stern words which had faced the congregation from on high (HOLY HOLY HOLY) had struck me as hideous.

All I found around me were walls of an airily refreshing colour – cream-emulsion – which, for me, were reminiscent of many a lime-washed Quaker meeting-house.

In my ignorance, I was about to leave the church and puzzle myself no further. Angela, some years before, had told me that German bombs had damaged three churches decorated by Tressell and left no trace of his work. She had told me that St Andrews had also been damaged, but didn't mention that the bomb had only destroyed one of Tressell's panels (the one above the altar). I wrongly concluded, therefore, that the entire chancel had been bombed and rebuilt.

But a fleeting gleam of common-sense made me feel for a coin in my pocket and give one of the walls a last-minute scratch.

Something else gleamed – gold-leaf. And then a rich blue. And then …

I'll leave Fred to give the official sequel in the way he thought best. But may I mention the historical source of my confusion? Unknown to me (after all, that was my busiest decade), St Andrew's church had been invaded by French students in 1967. They had daubed obscene slogans (in French) all over some of the panels as well as the pews. Angela had herself helped the President of the Anglo-French Club to compose a letter (in French) for publication in the local *Observer*. Her French was a lot better than mine and the slogans, she blandly told me, were extremely rude. The public reproach did nothing to reveal the culprits, but the historical result was that the vicar decided to re-decorate the entire chancel. The matter would thus have rested had I not scratched the wall because Fred, like everyone else, didn't connect the vandalism. (May I just add here that it was therefore rather illogical of Fred to blame Mr Pastry for not knowing what Fred himself didn't know.)

As I've already more than hinted, I was to wish that I could have avoided notifying Fred of this discovery. But obviously I had to notify him as well as (at Angela's suggestion) Mr Pastry.

May I remind you that I am referring to John Manwaring Baines? And please remember this. We must all pronounce the name "Manwaring" as "Mannering." It was Fred's failure to observe this social nicety that has put Fred beyond the pale. But Angela, I must also mention, regarded this social nicety as a hoot. She has always been merrily derisive about Mr Baines and his two well-honoured positions. One was his job as curator of the towns two museums; the other was his highly respected office as Parish Clerk to All Saints. She did not, however, ever refer to him – as I did – as Mr Pastry. She had always referred to him by his initials – JMB.

"You need to notify JMB" she had said, after I had told her of my coin-scratch. "He has a special trust-fund at his personal disposal. He can easily give you any reasonable sum to pay the demolishers for at least one panel. He doesn't regard Tressell as having much importance, but I shall tell him to pay up. The museum must step in. I'll insist."

Rather surprised by her confident assurance, I said: "Are you sure you have that much influence?"

"Of course I have," she chortled.

It goes to prove, I suppose, how unwise it is to marry someone too hastily and without knowing very much about them, but Angela was always able to surprise me about herself.

49

She went on to say: "The silly old fool is nuts about me. Always has been."

I was so surprised, indeed, that I naively uttered the time-honoured words: "But he's a married man …"

"David," said Angela, with patient condescension, "you really do have a lot to learn about local government officials. I've had to do a lot of fending off, and not only from JMB. But he's the most persistent. He even tried to get me to transfer to his staff just after the War."

This piece of gossip surprised me still further. I more-or-less gasped: "But surely you wouldn't be qualified to work in a museum?"

"Oh," she carelessly said, "he could have wangled it. He's wangled all sorts of things for me. But I turned that one down. I didn't want to spend the rest of my life being chased round the muniments."

I didn't know what muniments were (I had to look up the word in the dictionary); but there is no doubting the fact that, without this secret passion for Angela, the then curator would never have countenanced any relic of Robert Tressell.

"I'll make sure," she finally assured me, "that he puts you in total charge of the rescue-operation. In that way, I think, you'll reduce at least some of the trouble you're likely to get from Fred. But don't worry. I won't be sticking my nose in too obviously. I have other fish to fry."

I was only dimly beginning to see, at this time, why Kathleen was so fascinated by Angela's style of life; but I was too confounded by the fuss about the mural to weigh up two unpredictable women. STORM OVER PAINTINGS IN CHURCH ran one absurd headline, which increased the pressure on us all in preventing nightly thefts from the mural as well as uninvited callers at home. ("I appeal to you, in the name of Robert Tressell, to let me stay just one night. I'm not asking for breakfast, just a doss-down on the sofa.") Even the self-possessed Angela was reduced to panic

50

and tears by some of these unwelcome developments. She could only be propitiated by inclusion in the documentary film (in a re-enactment of Fred in the reference-library "researching" Robert Tressell). As for Mr Pastry, he was also upset, but, in his case, by the producer wishing to enact a scene in the modern-day museum (where Tressell had never trod). Mr Pastry pranced about crying: "Bogus! Bogus!" (He had only allowed the filming because he thought he was pleasing Angela.)

I regret to say that I only saw the film once, as did so many, because in those days there was no way of recording it for oneself. I can only recall that it was seven hours of costly film but cut down, for transmission, to about half an hour. (The search for this now missing film still goes on. All that remains of it are the shots I took myself, during the filming and which were also included in the main film itself.) I am not, I regret, able to remember much of the film or the order of scenes.

One moment, however, I do remember most vividly.

The producer, whose blushes I will spare by not naming him, offended Kathleen by uttering a certain sexual expletive. It is commonplace in television plays today; in 1970 it was considered low-class and unmentionable. Even Fred never uttered it, but the producer was getting rather vexed with having to film and re-film Fred and Kathleen walking arm-in-arm. He uttered the expletive. Joan, Kathleen's daughter, was immediately unable to suppress her frequently rebellious giggling. But Kathleen, of course, was genuinely shocked and became even more like Lady Bracknell.

As for me, I was only upset in the sense applied to any indecisive male. I made no headway whatsoever with Kathleen during my "interview" with her inside Fred's rather old motor-car. It took almost a whole morning to film this scene, with Fred supposedly driving us around the town – and looking like a sulky old Roman emperor. The BBC cameraman was in the passenger seat, beside Fred, but screwed around to film Kathleen and me in the back. (The sound-recordist was imprisoned very perilously in the boot, with about half an inch of open lid to prevent suffocation.) In transmission, the scene was cut down (I seem to recall) to little more than a few superficial seconds.

The whole tenor and theme of the film was, naturally enough, in support of the existing legend. At this stage, I still believed in it myself. Only a few mild flutterings of doubt affected me, these having been induced by various attempts by Reginald and Joan to get me on their side.

This state of mind was now to be widened.

I cannot guarantee the exact moment in time when I saw this inoffensive-looking man standing, on his own, amid the increasing piles of church-rubble. He wore a plain, gabardine raincoat. He had no hat. He didn't look particularly old, nor did he look in ill-health (although he was to die in a matter of months.) He certainly didn't look rich (although he was to leave £59,000, duty paid some £12,000. This was an enormous amount in those days and not to be sneezed at even now).

I had succeeded in placating Fred by encouraging him to select a goodish bit of spare mural for "making into a fire-screen" (which was what he was itching to do). Methylated spirit is excellent for cleaning off emulsion-paint, but death to gold-leaf. Having warned him of this and left him at work on his proposed fire-screen, I approached this hesitating stranger with only routine curiosity. I took him to be one of the church commissioners or other official visitors who (contrary to Fred's later account in *One of the Damned*) were always polite and as co-operative as their interests allowed.

"Are you Mr Haines?" he asked, so quietly and awkwardly as to seem furtive.

"Yup, yup," I breezily replied.

"I've just been in to see Mrs Haines at the library," he said, almost whispering. "I'm from over the road – from Burton's."

He was referring to Burton's the Builders whose firm, still in existence, was almost opposite the church in Queen's Road (a main thoroughfare in central Hastings). He was the now the firm's owner, but the mural had been a memorial to the original owner's mother. (Fred doesn't mention this in his account.) The firm had also been one of the firms which, according to Fred, had treated Tressell so abominably. Without bothering to think, I said (and still breezily): "Is it Mr Ball you'd like to see? I can take you over to him."

"No, no," he hurriedly mumbled. "It's only you I think I need to see. It's just to tell you that we got rid of all the original drawings and stencils only a few weeks ago. We didn't realise what they really were. But Mrs Haines suggests you might like to come in, with her, to look over some of our other records. There might still be something of interest to you when all this," he said, with a really furtive glance around, "has died down …"

He didn't say whether or not he had encountered Fred in person, but, it seemed to me, that he was anxious to avoid the possibility. My sympathies were at once aroused. I thanked him (in much the same furtive manner as his) and began asking him just a few questions about Tressell's terms of employment.

"Oh," said this man, whose name was Mr Farmer, "he wasn't like the chap in the book he wrote. Seems he often worked independently. More a sub-contractor as you might say. He worked all over the town and was in demand – he wasn't a labourer. A lot of people wanted him to work for them – not just in churches. A big job like the oriental café probably got him more work than he could take on. His work got a lot of attention."

Having been so imbued with the legend of Tressell's poverty and deprivation, I found this information hard to absorb. (I've condensed it from the succession of remarks Mr Farmer made in those few hurried moments.)

I asked a few questions about the way Tressell might have organised the painting of such a massive mural. From the way Fred had spoken of it, I had imagined Tressell having to lug his own ladder around and working, half-starved, in candlelight (as well as "arguing with the verger about the existence of God," and, of course, being paid next to nothing.) Even from the few details Mr Farmer gave me about the high scaffolding and lighting needed, I began to feel my picture of Tressell changing. I could feel it changing, right there in that now ruined church.

I also felt a little ridiculous. How on earth could I have been so stupid as to not realise that Frank Owen, in the book, is not in any way depicted as painting churches on such a massive scale? And how could I ever have imagined Tressell writing a massive book – in his "spare" time – while having to organise his "other" massive work all over the town? In depicting the character of Frank Owen, assumed by so many to be a self-portrait, Tressell had used only a fraction of his own work-experience as the basis. Mr Farmer left me stunned, but he hurried away, I think it correct to guess, without knowing it.

He seemed, in my opinion, to be a very kindly man with good intentions in having sought me out, but I thought it wise only to mention the loss of the sketches and stencils to Fred. I did so as tactfully as possible and Fred said: "The bastard should have known bloody better," yet he was, oddly, relatively calm. I was thankful that his response was merely as automatic as a dyspeptic grunt.

I would like, at this stage of this memoir, to mention just one of the deeper Tressellian values, which I was only too slowly becoming aware of.

It is that writing, as a career, is (or should be) an act of public friendship. It quite simply shouldn't be anything else. Although Tressell's life was short, I believe that writing could have become his career and that he would have exemplified that value (among many others). In trying to follow that value in my own very patchy career, I can only claim that I regret having to upset certain readers – as I know I will – who cannot venture beyond the legend. I don't know if Fred ever learnt of the later researches by others into Tressell's prison sentence in Liverpool and his "sordid" divorce from his wife. I haven't, myself, checked on these colourful discoveries and, on balance, I hope that neither Fred nor Kathleen ever found out about them. I can only tell you that I have seen tears in Fred's eyes as he spoke of the sufferings Tressell endured. And tears in the eyes of Kathleen when she spoke of missing the mother she couldn't recall but was told had died of typhoid in Africa. But the point has to be made at this stage of this memoir: it is because of those shifting sands beneath the legend that both Fred and Kathleen were so often so unknowingly difficult – as well as knowingly! I am not in any way discounting "colourful" discoveries, but, for those who do, it can only be a major upset to hear that Robert Tressell and Robert Noonan were two very separate people. One was real and one was not.

And, I suggest, we are only likely to find the real Tressellian values (including the ultimate value) in the real Robert.

The sort of human being who would be upset by any change in the legend would probably be like the anonymous enthusiast who wrote to us enclosing a pound note and a ten-shilling note. Fred was very moved and touched by this letter and so was I. He quotes it in full in his biography, but I quote from it here in support of my differing point (as well as to illustrate my perplexity).

> Dear Young Philanthropists,
>
>   Thank you for trying to preserve something of Tressell's. The quality of his work as an artist is not important – the quality of his mind and values is what matters. … there will always be those who will love and respect this darling iconoclast … together we will remember and salute Robert Tressell …

Fred, then over 65, stood repeating "this darling iconoclast" with the dreamiest look on his face that I ever seen while the only "young" philanthropist on the site was Fred's daughter Clare, aged ten. As Fred very aptly comments, it was probably the press pictures including Clare which inspired the donation "to buy something to ease those dry and dusty throats." He was to get several human details wrong in his account (such as implying that Angela and our two sons were helping us, which was never the case,) but he showed so much heart over this adoring letter that I knew it impossible for me ever to discuss Mr Farmer's impression. (Fred also repeated words from the letter about the pauper's grave, his voice trembling.)

After all, I told myself, Mr Farmer could have been mistaken. And there was no doubting the burial in the pauper's grave, was there? And, as it turned out, Angela and I were never to join Mr Farmer in exploring other records.

I can't recall exactly when it was, but I was walking in Claremont with Angela (the quiet little backwater which included not only the public library but the huge west-side of Holy Trinity, Angela's church).

"Good Heavens," I said. "Look at that!"

An Edwardian type of funeral *cortège* was entering Claremont – black horses with plumes and all the jingling trimmings. I had not seen such a grandiose sight since my childhood in pre-war London.

"Who on earth is getting this send-off," I coarsely asked, and she replied: "Mr Farmer."

She had come out of the library and was joining me for a cup of tea somewhere, and said nothing more except, a month or two later, when she told me how much money Mr Farmer had left behind him. (Such snippets were all grist for her many scrap-books.)

I regret to say that some ten more years were to pass before anything more was done about the one panel I had chosen for spiritual enlightenment of the town. As Fred's book was to say (in 1973), the panel had to be hacked off the wall at some speed and the numbered shards put into a set of cardboard boxes (from the nearest supermarket). Angela then took them into care at the library. Understandably, Fred was never to know that she had soon insisted that Mr Baines should take them. They were therefore transferred to the museum's back-street depot (in Waterworks Road) where, frankly, they would have stayed (probably mouldering into further disintegration) had not Mrs Irene Wright popped up (ten years later).

Hats off to this Tressell enthusiast from London is all we can say now.

Had she not been shocked to discover nothing more had been done and had she not at once set about organising a restoration-appeal, I think it likely that this last piece of surviving work would have been lost. I took some film-shots of her supervising the removal of the boxes from the depot, but I cannot absolve myself from my own laggardly behaviour. Worse still, I have to confess that I even forgot to contribute to the Appeal! My excuse is that I had been so exhausted by the whole operation and was subsequently so busy that I could only think back on it in a mood of distaste and even actual depression.

The best that can be said of such a mood was that it did help me to understand how Tressell himself must have sometimes experienced "burn-out" of this type. Without wishing to blame the trade-union authorities (and even Socialists among those who regard themselves as Christian-Socialists), I still sometimes reflect that their better help could have relieved us. More than one panel out of the sixteen could have been saved, perhaps for installing in Christian-Socialist premises elsewhere (even a church or two). I can only add that even atheistic Socialists of the intellectual type were human. Even they did wince ("Oh, no!") when I showed the film of the pick-axe going through the remaining panels. But Kathleen's reaction I couldn't understand. She seemed curiously unmoved by that bit of film. It was to take me ten or twelve more years before I understood why.

Today, you can buy postcards from the museum of the mural-panel, but, really, the miraculous nature of the restoration is only evident in an enlargement of the kind Mrs Wright sent to me. Tressell's gold-leaf and roses (symbols of love) only give you the full effect, in a good light, of the glittering original if you see a sufficiently large picture. It was not designed as a miniature, any more that it was designed for an inadequately-lit photograph in tones of black-and-white.

Had there not been a second world war, we would have had a lot more of Tressell's work surviving in Hastings; as it is, this one panel is a good example of Edwardian church-painting which any museum would be glad to exhibit. I even found the symbols of fidelity under the emulsion-paint in one low corner of the chancel. Although hardly likely to have been all that visible in 1905, these symbols were carefully if not perfectly executed. (Do I need to say what they were?)

It was only belatedly that I saw how all this prodigious work illustrates another Tressellian value: namely, the fundamental desire of human beings to do a good job of work if they are given the chance. Tressell was probably the first writer to show us, in the RTP, the pathos of those workers who, out of their own money, secretly bought sandpaper in the hope of imparting a proper finish to the wood they were ordered to daub.

I also saw, belatedly, the sort of inner conflict Tressell probably experienced in wanting to do different types of mural-work (which demanded all his attention) and the desire to get on with his writing (which also demanded his full attention). I also found that I was able to identify with this conflict myself – as many other writers have. In other words, in working in that chancel, I was beginning to re-kindle my love for my former workshop in Wellington Mews (where I had tried to set up my own woodwork-business). I was beginning to smell the lure of the wood-shavings and the smell of shellac. You who may know nothing of such things cannot imagine how enticing the smell of shellac and wood-stain can be! It competed seductively with the beckoning impulse to write. Tressell, I daresay, also experienced the crass ignorance of those who advise: 'No problem. Why not just do the writing in your spare time? It's only a matter of sitting down at a typewriter – or even just writing with a Biro.'

I don't know if Fred ever revised his own first opinion of the panel ("Let's face it, it's no Picasso …"), but he was still so inclined to bear a grudge against Mr Baines that a coolness stayed between us. By the time he was finishing the new biography a year or two later, we were only on uneasy speaking terms. I'm sorry to say that I didn't really help him when he rang, one day, to ask me to clarify details about the salvage (for his chapter forty). I had tried to inform him of the pronounciation of the name Manwaring, but, in the biography, he "got his own back" by spelling the name wrongly. Like many an estrangement, ours had a trivial basis, which is difficult to recall but seemed even to include the letter, from Mr Baines, which I had foolishly showed to Fred.

Since it was to have ironic consequences in other ways (and not least the careless relegation of the remnants), I quote that letter here. Note the date. It was written before Mr Baines retired in 1973 (the date Fred published the biography) and before Mr Baines became a long-standing and jovial visitor to our council flat. He was to become virtually a family friend, with one of our offspring teasing Angela by chantingly calling him 'Bainsey-Boy.' Fred, be it noted, is not mentioned in this urbane letter of thanks. (Upon such omissions does many a friendship become unstuck. I was siding, you see, with the enemy.)

> 29th September, 1970
> Dear Mr Haines,
>
> We had a meeting of the Museum & Art Gallery Committee last night, when I made a full report on the Robert Tressell paintings in St Andrews Church, and I told them of your most successful rescue-operation. It is absolutely certain that without your very kind assistance

nothing would have been saved, and the town is the richer for it. The time will undoubtedly come when there will be a very great interest in this unhappy man, and for the Museum to possess some of his work will be a very great advantage.

My Committee asked me to express to you their most sincere thanks for all you have done, and to this I would like to add my own. Would you be good enough to thank your wife and the other members of her staff who helped.

Kind regards,

Yours sincerely,

J. MANWARING BAINES,

Curator.

I saved and personally restored just two minor Tressell relics (minor, I mean, compared with the importance of the panel). Both were to cause me still more world-weary groans.

The first was a rose-motif from the right-hand wall (as seen in the gloomy photograph of the original work). It was virtually intact, I having worked upon it in situ. Carefully, I wrapped it and sent it off to Kathleen. I was soon to be heavily dismayed by a subsequent letter from her. It revealed that she had "tried to touch up the rose with gold paint," and "had seemed to spoil it." (Gold paint? Ugh!)

The second relic had rather more complex consequences for my weak political allegiance.

At just a small amount of risk (small, yes, but risk nevertheless), I removed the Crown of Peace (Tressell's version) from high above an alcove in the chancel.

It was slightly but endearingly out of true. This prompted me, incidentally, to ask Kathleen if her father had ever worn spectacles. She replied that his eyesight was perfect and that she had never seen him wear anything other than sun-glasses. (She also said he had "lovely teeth.")

This time, I got another Fred (Mr Fred Buss, a Desert-Rat veteran and a sign-writer/decorator AND a life-long Labour supporter) to restore the crown. (It had got damaged, despite my best efforts.) Like the Philanthropists who bought their own sandpaper, I bought and paid for the gold-leaf out of my own pocket. I also supplied the other necessary materials, including a stout wood-base. On completion, I offered the whole article to the local Labour party.

I had heard they were setting up a new headquarters (at that time in Wellington Square). Tressell's Crown, I thought, would add a nice finishing touch.

I received an incredibly Stalinist letter which more-or-less demanded that I should hand over the crown immediately. I even had a phone call which seemed to imply I was in possession of property I had stolen. Having met far more perfectly pleasant Labour people, such as the unfortunate Councillor Ted, I managed to stay philosophic. I complied. But neither Fred Buss nor I were invited to this HQ ceremony. I can't recall the date, but it was attended by Mr Neil Kinnock, now the ennobled Lord Kinnock. I seem to have seen a photograph somewhere of Fred Ball doing the honours but looking like a corked volcano. Fred was always explosive on the subject of professional politicians. I was less explosive but it's why I can't join the Labour Party.

And I don't think I'm alone in this feeling of political reserve. But it's for others, I suggest, to consider whether Tressell would have admired the Labour Party of today.

My own experience was not, as is said today, a one-off. Example: I once tried to get help from the Labour party in trying to obtain hygienic improvements for the council-estate where Fred Ball and I were still living. I was rather curtly told, over the phone, that "since you are not a member of the party, we can't help you," and Fred, whom I must have been in better touch with, growlingly said: "That's typical of bloody Labour in this bloody town. Tressell's too good for them."

Where is the Tressell Crown today? I have no idea. At one time, it seemed to have drifted into the possession of the public library – propped up on a filing-cabinet.

Angela herself had no explanation and was increasingly taking less and less interest in the mural other than as an opportunity for a joke or two. This became more obvious in 1974 when she ceased being the Borough Reference Librarian and was promoted boss of the library in Bexhill, a town a little further along the coast.

On one of her sunny days off, Angela and I were being driven by Mr Pastry in his car over Romney Marsh just beyond Hastings. (We had no car until 1980). I was alone in the back and Angela was in the front beside Mr Pastry. Casting a wickedly covert backward glance at me, she said to Mr Pastry (whom she must have known had forgotten I was on board): "What on earth has happened to all that Tressell stuff in Waterworks Road?"

"I don't know, my dear," he replied, "and I don't care. I've told Devenish" (the new curator) "that he should dump the lot. As for that bogus film they made, I can only hope it goes the same way," and he chuckled cynically.

I was so miffed that I ignored the fact that a deep ditch was to one side of us. After a second or two, I loudly and deliberately said (in reference to our destination, New Romney): "Are we nearly there?"

The startled Mr Pastry jolted twistingly for a split-second. He then drove almost straight into the ditch, wrestling with the wheel in no comical fashion. Drivers have been drowned going into those ditches on Romney Marsh. We ended up with the front bumper almost over the water. He was in such a bad state of shock and embarrassment that I took pity on him and pretended to have been asleep.

"What's happened? Have we gone and crashed or something? I must have nodded off …"

Looking subdued but relieved, he recovered the situation without any damage other than one mud-clogged front wheel. He himself made a joke about having tried to drown us, but it was, actually, a very serious near-accident. It left Angela shivering, as well it might, but she, too, soon recovered from our joint act of folly.

Having survived possible death on Romney Marsh, I was now in for a lot more friendly trouble from "the Tressells" for some six years.

FIVE

Kathleen and the First Tressell Lecture

I

Having failed to get me to influence the writing of Fred's new biography, the three Tressells now conspired (can there be any other word?) to prevail upon me in a more subtle way.

I resisted for all of six years.

Now that the new biography had been well-published (and well-received), the idea now was that I should give a public lecture to "counter-act" the inaccuracies. Although I had not been invited to see the biography at the "proofing" stage, I was surprised to learn that Kathleen had been allowed a glimpse but, to a very large extent, had "gone along" with many of the facts she was now disputing. She had, in a word, temporised. Yet she was now portraying herself to me (in her letters) as frustrated and furious.

Because of this inconsistency but also my reluctance to hurt Fred's feelings, I did my discreet best to stave off this new approach.

But Kathleen did not accompany the other Tressells (Joan and Reginald) when they came to my flat behind Fred's back. (Date unknown.) Complacently and foolishly, because she was a rising eighty-two, I thought Kathleen would this time be relatively harmless and easy to handle. The staving off, I reasoned, would be child's play – especially with Kathleen in faraway Bristol.

I must tell you that I liked Joan Johnson, Tressell's granddaughter. She was engagingly forthright about the shortcomings of the Labour party and the Trade Unions (which didn't gain her a lot of popularity) and, to this day, I regret that our acquaintance didn't blossom into an abiding friendship. The main reason was that I was so busy with excitingly varied projects to do with the spoken word on tape. I had no time to absorb the fact that Joan didn't have her mother's iron constitution. Having suffered rheumatic fever as a child, Joan had a weak heart and was often unwell.

As for Reginald, we would never have heard of Joan or Kathleen had it not been for him. He was undoubtedly the prime mover. Without his "interference" (as Fred angrily called it), I would not now be writing this memoir and would certainly never have given what came to be known as the "first" Tressell lecture.

The reference to it being "the first" is only by the fact of it being the first in Hastings (as far as anyone knew), as well as being the first of several more lectures as a sequel (in Hastings). For reasons which will become apparent, I became reluctant to give any further lectures on Tressell. These subsequent lectures were given by other people such as Tony Benn and other leading lights of the Labour movement. The Workers' Educational Association, for whom I gave the "first" lecture, were surprised by the audience-figures for the "first" lecture; this inspired the WEA to set up more "Tressell lectures" as an annual event.

The "first" lecture was soon forgotten and the annual lectures eventually petered out, but, as far as I know, all supported the legend. I didn't much mind. For me, even in my own lecture, the idea of opposing the legend was distasteful.

It would hurt too many feelings, let alone those of poor old Fred. What harm could it do the readers if they believed Robert Tressell and Frank Owen to be indentical?

And why spoil a good joke by demolishing the myth that Mugsborough was Hastings? Tressell had made it clear enough (in a postscript) that he was not portraying a seaside-town. He was too good a writer not to have included the prevailing atmosphere of the sea – and the local fishing industry – if he had meant Mugsborough to resemble Hastings. A little bit of ignorance on this point, for many readers, was all part of the book's attractiveness. It couldn't possibly harm the real town itself – in fact, it could be said to bring it additional fame. Thus did I rationalise my moral diffidence.

I was alone in the flat when Joan and Husband Reg turned up, uninvited, without Kathleen. I'm sorry to say I crushed down my sympathies for them and gave them a hard time. They had various letters and documents with them, plus a copy of *One of the Damned* annotated by Kathleen in many a margin.

"We know you do a lot of lecturing," said Reginald. "All we're suggesting is a lecture where you could show your film of the mural, together with some slides of the town when my grandfather-in-law was living here."

He called Tressell his grandfather-in-law!

I felt swamped, but I sat looking through the annotated copy with all the snooty detachment of an Old Bailey judge.

Joan said encouragingly: "Mum says you can use her notes in any way you like. You can make them a part of the lecture."

Reginald: "She also agrees it would be a very good idea if you were to have a special talk with her – all on your own. A really private talk."

"Yes," added Joan, giggling, "and to be honest I think she'll tell you a lot more than she tells even me!"

Reginald: "It will be exclusive information, David. You're still someone we still trust."

"Trust for what reason," I remember the Old Bailey judge aloofly asking.

"In service of the truth," said Reginald, turning prim and pink, "if you agree to give the lecture. My wife doesn't want her grandfather being used as propaganda for class-hatred like Fred's. Her grandfather was not all that much a victim of capitalism. Class-hatred is a sin."

To my acute embarrassment, Joan turned more than suddenly serious. She said: "All I want is my grandfather to be remembered as a normal but gentle-minded human being," and she burst into tears.

I'm ashamed to this day that I cruelly said: "It's not for me to judge, but I would say your grandfather was far from normal. In my opinion, he was so remarkable as to be beyond assessment. His talents alone will always make him a mystery."

As miserably as a stricken child, she said: "Why are you being so horrible? We always thought you were a nice man."

Guiltily irritated, I said: "People should be left to make up their own minds. What is it you want me to do? Make out that your grandfather was a liar? And your mother too," I very nearly added but managed to stop myself. "Many of these annotations strike me as inconsistent," was what I said instead.

"You're the only one who can iron them out," said Joan, mopping away her tears but still upset.

Really sternly, I said: "You think I should interview your mother before I give the lecture, is that it?"

"We think it's important," sniffed Joan.

"And can I expect her," I said, "to explain away the title-page of your grandfather's novel? Does it not say – and clearly – told by one of the damned and set down by Robert Tressell?"

Joan's reply was so extraordinary that it completely knocked me off my high horse.

She said: "Mum can't explain why he called himself one of the damned, nor can we. You're the only one who will be able to – and to explain why it's such a bad title for Fred's book."

"But it's a brilliant title," I feebly protested.

"Well I don't like it," said Joan, as snappingly as her mother at her worst. "But, since Fred has chosen to use it, I can suggest a good title for your lecture. You should call it *Not One of the Damned.*"

She had stood up to say this, as if to denote her final word – in the way that ladies often do.

Breathlessly, if not gaspingly, I staggered to my feet and said: "I can't possibly deliver a lecture, probably with old Fred in the front row, with a title of that sort!"

"Then you are at least agreeing to do the lecture," said Joan, as quickly as a blow-dart.

"Well, yes, it might be nice to show films of the mural stuff," I weakly conceded, "and perhaps just make a few comments to iron out a few things …"

This earned me a kiss on the cheek and a big smile, and, from Reginald, a hearty handshake. I was beaten. I knew it, but I was to hold them off for upwards of six years, as I have said – a marvel of procrastination if I may say so.

Actually, the marvel was not that hard to achieve for someone as busy as myself and busy, moreover, in one of the most fascinating (and even glamorous) decades. I was setting up a drama-recording group in Hastings (a development-group, not a production-company); and, through this and magazine-articles I was publishing, I was meeting talented and interesting people. Also, in joining various technical associations, I was going on conferences to learn about mixers and other types of advanced recording-equipment. At the same time, I was involved with bodies such as the local community-service council in bidding (unsuccessfully, alas) for a local-radio franchise. For these and other good reasons, I can't altogether remember the chronology of even my most vivid memories.

It's a common saying that our memories play tricks on us, but I believe this saying to be wrong. It is we who play tricks on our memories, but how and why can often be impossible to work out. I've been able, therefore, only to give you a very mixed bag of memories concerning the way I was finally brought to heel by the three Tressells.

By 1980 (a whole ten years since the mural-rescue,) I had finally put together a WEA lecture for a fee of £20.

Quaintly, the WEA announced it as a Day-School, beginning at two in the afternoon on May 3rd (my birthday!) and ending at six in the evening. The title I had chosen, in mild defiance of Tressell's grand-daughter, was THE STRANGE CASE OF ROBERT TRESSELL. I had borrowed this title, in part, from the well-known story of Dr Jekyll and Mr Hyde (that classical portrayal of split-personality). I was careful, however, not to emphasise this meaning too much – especially with Fred in the audience, and, as I had gloomily predicted, almost in the front row.

Also, and this has been kept a secret until now, a plot was hatched to avoid upsetting Fred. It had to look as if the lecture had been offered to Fred first, rather than to me, and that I took it on only after he (for health-reasons as well as stage-fright) had turned it down.

But there was a second very odd aspect to these arrangements. At the time, I couldn't understand how it happened, but the interview with Kathleen, which had been scheduled beforehand, was delayed. It was now to take place, in Bristol, after the lecture. I merely assumed that an old lady in her late eighties had genuine reasons for: (a) being unable to attend the lecture; and (b) for not being available until June for the "deep" interview. (Memo to younger Tressellians: it is only when you're in your eighties yourself, if you stay fit and frisky, that you'll realise how other fit and frisky eighty-year olds can be so full of guile.)

Expecting only a smallish audience, the WEA booked only the public library's own very smallish lecture-room behind a pub in Robertson Street. (It used to be the town-centre's police-station.)

To everyone's astonishment, including mine, we had at least seventy people crowding in – with more, in mid-afternoon, getting in for nothing and having to stand. Some, it turned out, had come from distant parts of the country, armed with portable tape-recorders. The attraction, needless to say, was not myself but the subject-matter and the promise of film and slides. It was, I have to state, a unique occasion, and not least for the feeling I had of walking a tight-rope across Niagara Falls. But the confrontation I had expected from the "extreme left-wingers" as mentioned by Reginald failed to materialise.

He and Joan sat well apart from Fred and beamed at me benevolently. The atmosphere was happy and friendly. It was full of tolerance for my cautious references to the inconsistencies of legend – and in particular the matter of Tressell's death and burial. The only fly in the ointment, I am really sorry to say, was Fred. He was really the only one present who wasn't happy. It was only having his wife Jacquie, beside him, which seemed to be holding his ire within bounds. Yet I was doing what I damn well could to avoid upsetting him. I was even censoring myself – as my notes for the lecture could prove. (I have them in front of me as I compose this chapter.) I had gone through them and crossed out all the deeper stuff, which I thought would upset him but which, had he not attended, I would have included.

And that would have included Dr Davy's opinion about the hospital-death in far more detail. In those days, your family doctor was more likely to be someone involved in the life of the town and often to be met at social events. Angela had long before asked for his opinion and he had given her a memo to take down. This was now a delicate subject because, after the BBC had filmed the burial-site in 1970, a memorial stone of Swedish granite had been emplaced – which Joan, among so many others, had witnessed in 1977. The medical opinion in no way belittles that ceremony, but, to someone like Fred, it would do so. Another problem for me, at the time of the lecture, was that I had yet to learn of what really happened when Kathleen was told of her father's death. I had to skirt around that aspect of the matter like an astronaut having to skirt around a black hole in outer space.

I didn't even mention Dr Davy by name. I only referred to "a doctor" being consulted. It only had value, of course, in being just one doctor's opinion, but he was local and he knew the score.

Even today, Dr Davy's opinion is not going to be understood if readers cannot accept that Fred was wrong in stating (as he does in his preface) that Tressell "died in 1911 at the age of forty in the Walton Workhouse, Liverpool."

Fred refused to alter this statement and, in the lecture, even seemed to grind his teeth when I touched upon this unsupported assertion. The simple truth is that Tressell was admitted to hospital from his lodgings in Erskine Street, Liverpool. Kathleen had sent me, in a letter, details of an official letter she had received which confirmed Fred was wrong. But it's amazing that so many people, despite this clarity, still believe in Fred's workhouse – and therefore death from destitution.

"Absolute tosh," is how Dr Davy expressed himself more colloquially in describing Fred's belief that Tressell's health was identical with that of the fictitious Frank Owen.

The belief that Tressell daily spat blood but his family didn't care enough to notice is totally inane, but it's what I believed myself. It proves how ignorant I was (as are so many) of what it takes to write a long novel as well as paint enormous murals. Both forms of endeavour demand not just skill but strength and stamina of a very high order.

"Painting a mural," a professional artist told me, furthering Mr Farmer's comments, "isn't just a matter of a step-ladder and a paint-pot. It's tough going and you need to be more than just a decorator."

It took that particular artist three years to paint the famous murals at Fort Lympne. He had painted murals for a Maharajah in India, and, as a Hastings man, had seen Tressell's restaurant-murals in his youth and had admired them.

Try as I might, I cannot remember the date of this advice. I only know that it was on the occasion of a small dinner-party which Arthur (the artist) gave for both Angela and me. And the only reason I remember the occasion, I have to admit, is because Arthur's invitation had an ulterior motive. He was hoping that Angela could be persuaded to pose in the nude. His mention of murals was just small-talk.

In that day and age, posing nude was a shocking proposition, but Arthur was the soul of tact. Leaving the unsuspecting Angela with his quietly mischievous wife, he took me into his studio. It was here that he had painted Mrs Catherine Cookson (but not in the nude) and what she had said to him, during the sitting, was to be unspokenly central to my lecture.

He began showing me his girly-nudes (as his wife cheerfully called them). Although no expert on nudes or indeed painting, I thought them pretty good and the proposition a compliment to Angela.

"I think it best to ask if you don't mind," he said, "and if you, yourself, will sound her out on your way home. I'm not touting for a fee, I hope you realise. I simply crave to paint your wife. She has that inner quality of femininity, which is so essential to the painting of the nude. Purely for exhibition."

In my ignorance, I regret to say I mis-heard. I thought he had said "inequality of femininity" rather than "inner quality" and this was to be a big mistake.

Nice old Arthur had very kindly laid on a hired car (with a properly-garbed chauffeur) to take us back to our council-estate, and that fellow's ears must have been flapping and his eyes bulging.

"Why on earth," Angela almost yelled, "couldn't Arthur have asked me when I was younger? I'm still proud of my body, but it isn't what it was – not for posing in the nude for a good-looking man."

"It's not so much the body he wants to paint," I clumsily tried to explain, "but the feminine inequality of the body – compared with men, I suppose."

This didn't go down well either, and I had to phone Arthur and tell him of her refusal (putting it politely, of course). He, being a very nice chap, took it well and didn't persist. I can only be grateful to him for his professional information about mural-painting and for what he had said, over dinner, about Mrs Cookson. Even if no one else were to accept my thesis, his information was among all the aspects of the Tressell saga which were helping me to discover what I think of as "deeper" Tressellian values.

II

And what was my thesis? And how had Mrs Cookson unknowingly helped me to begin shaping it?

She had poured out her heart to Arthur, but he only spoke of her other terrible problems some twelve of so years later. The matter he spoke of relating to my lecture was her possession of the 1955 edition of the RTP (with its sub-title).

She had apparently told Arthur (and in a passion I can easily imagine) that Tressell's description of himself as one of the damned "could only mean one thing."

It was bastardy, she declared, and she used that term fiercely and not the more genteel term. She told Arthur that she knew what it was like to be damned because, being a bastard, she was damned.

Mrs Cookson, be it noted, had known extreme poverty herself and had been a victim of it, but she was apparently furious at the thought that anyone could believe or say that poverty alone meant damnation. The RTP sub-title, she had said, was eyewash.

I would have liked to have taken up this opinion with Mrs Cookson myself, but I would never have had the nerve. I do remember the painting of her in her drawing-room (the whole room was full of photographs of herself and lined with runs of her books, like a bookshop), but I never checked whether that was Arthur's painting or not. I can only assume it was, and today I have no idea what happened to it. I only remember it as an imperious likeness (which, frankly, I didn't care for as a work of art). My very last meeting with her was at the Stables Theatre where I saw her standing at the top of the stairs, near the doors to the balcony-seats. She looked miserable, alone and ignored. It was the only time I had ever seen her in the theatre and I had no idea why she was there. We exchanged just a few words. She told me she was thinking "going back up North" and that the very thought made her feel literally sick. I said that Arnold Bennett (the novelist) was said to have had the same symptoms about the North but got over it. She just stared into my face, her lips moving but saying no more. Politely, I hope, I drifted away. I can still see her.

I can't remember when this last meeting occurred, but it must have been well before the lecture. It remains vivid and that's all. But I never mentioned her at the lecture because: (a) the information was private and about a living person; and (b) I had yet to get more details out of Kathleen about her father's death and burial.

I think I touched upon the Cookson interpretation of "one of the damned" but, perhaps, so delicately that only Fred was bristlingly aware of it.

I was only a shade more positive about the death and burial, keeping Angela's casual memo on Dr Davy well out of sight. (Angela, by the way, did not attend the lecture. She only came in as we were finishing in the late afternoon.)

I could only speak theoretically, therefore, in saying that Tressell's burial "as a pauper" was probably accidental. I didn't even dare look at Fred as I said so, but several in the audience were inclined to agree. One gentleman put it a lot more boldly than I and another declared that it was all "as interesting as a play." This led to an exciting finish and I was applauded without any dissent, although I don't know if Fred Ball applauded or not. I had made a point of ending by praising his biography for its very real qualities, but I can't deny that I hoped this would mollify him.

I quite thought my sly tactic had succeeded.

In some exhaustion, I was packing up my projector and films. Joan and Reginald were proffering their plaudits at my elbow. (I had been kept on my feet well beyond the nominal time, but I was gratified by the enthusiasm.)

Unsmilingly, Fred interrupted the plaudits to say: "What's going on?" and he added in the same breath: "I think all us lot deserve a drink after that marathon."

He domineeringly led the way out to the pub a few yards away in Robertson Street. Naturally, my fellow conspirators and I thought we were being regarded as his celebrity guests. But I should have known, from my tea-shop experience way back in 1962, that invitations from Fred were not always free. Selecting the table for us to sit at and including Angela and his own wife in the invitation, he grandly ordered the drinks. After their arrival, he made us all stump up. ("I could have died," his wife was to say to me afterwards. She had much to put up with, but she was always loyal and he had pointedly excluded her from the reimbursement-ritual.)

This occasion, I think, was the last time I had any contact with him face to face. He was yet to make that last phone-call (quoted at the start of this memoir) where he threatens to expose Kathleen in a "secret" paper. I have to say that my friendship was otherwise so cool that I, distracted by other interests, hardly even heard of him after the lecture. And Kathleen had already been saying in her letters that "we seldom hear from Fred now." I don't know if he ever knew that I was to interview her, but I think I should mention, at this stage of my memoir, that no trace so far has been found of the "secret" paper. Miss Cathy Walling, today's museum-curator, recently (2017) looked through the Fred Ball archive of 231 items and didn't find it.

I'm hoping he never wrote such a paper.

III

"Due to medical negligence," said Dr Davy.

He was chatting to me, glass in hand, at a party in a house very near to the two houses where Kathleen's aunt had run a school-refuge for blind children. He was chatting about the memo he had dictated to Angela (about Tressell's death in 1911), but this chat was a long time before the lecture. (I can't give a date.)

To understand this medical opinion yourself, you may need to appreciate that I had already recorded some "conversations" with Kathleen. (I can hardly describe them as interviews.) There were only two or three, I think, and they were so superficial and even banal that I re-used the cassettes. She simply didn't seem able to commit herself on tape as fully as I had hoped. Often, she would only give out deeper titbits when annoyed.

And often not all that privately. To go back to the BBC filming in 1970, during an interval when we were filming inside the former flat in Milward Road, I asked her what the designs were like which Fred had told me her father had painted on the floor (because he was too poor to buy proper carpets). Snapping me up in front of everyone, she said: "You're talking rubbish."

Fred's information derived, in the main, from one William Gower who, according to Kathleen, was not as intimate a friend of her father's as Fred had been led to believe. Yet Fred seems to have believed every single "fact" which Gower told him. I can remember Kathleen telling Fred that her father disliked coffee and only drank tea, but Fred preferred to believe Gower. He would not alter the story of how Gower and Tressell always drank pots and pots of coffee. I even said myself to Fred: "But wouldn't coffee be too expensive for a man as poor as Tressell to brew and drink in such quantities?"

Let me say that I think Kathleen was a little too hard on William Gower and his testimonies. She was ready enough to be tolerant towards those who, after the passage of two world wars, had distorted memories of Tressell when some of them were boys, and, moreover, had very simplistic reactions to a work of fiction. But Gower she would not forgive. Romancing and hyperbole were all right for herself, but not, it would seem, for Fred's primary witness. I can only suppose that it was Fred's blind faith in Gower that increased her fury with Gower. And perhaps the two world-famous photographs taken by Gower did earn justifiable credit with Fred, yet, according to Kathleen, Gower was not all that frequent a visitor. He was a local theatre-electrician and obviously very intelligent, but he often got his facts so wrong as to be ludicrous. One of them was that Tressell did his writing "sitting on a pile of books" because he was too poor to afford furniture. (His "desk" was an up-ended box.)

"Have YOU ever tried to sit on a pile of books and write?" Kathleen angrily asked me.

But that is the legend that still persists, along with other details by Gower and others about Tressell's poverty and therefore "inevitable" death.

Here is a brief account of those details. I shall then use Kathleen's annotations of Fred's biography to make Dr Davy's opinion of medical negligence more understandable. (Please bear in mind that Fred's innocently over-eager informants had no fear of rebuttal. They had no idea that Kathleen would so inconveniently pop up in 1967.)

Tressell, having fallen ill from over-work and lack of money to sustain him, had quarrelled with his sister, Adelaide. She had left him we are told, because of his Socialist principles. She would no longer "keep house" for him and left him and his daughter to endure their life of increasing poverty and ill-health together. We all saw something of this ghastly existence in a subsequent BBC drama-documentary entitled *Give Us this Day*. In it, we saw Kathleen trudging off to the soup-kitchen with a white enamel jug for the daily sustenance. ("David," she was to say to me, in some embarrassment after this film was shown, "I have never been in a Hastings soup-kitchen in my life.")

Having by now little or no possessions, her father now finally decided to end their days in Hastings in a few mean and cheaper rooms in the main road known as London Road. (A plaque now marks this one last dwelling.) He had resolved he would emigrate, with Kathleen, to Canada. But, first, this meant that he would travel to faraway Liverpool to earn money for the fare.

Nobody was able to explain why an educated man who, as they were often eager to state, could speak seven languages would seek work in Liverpool. But that's the story and I, at first, believed it myself. It is still being said, and believed, that he had tried going to London for work, but, after trudging the streets, had to return to Hastings in despair. ("He only went to London," Kathleen rather wearily told me, "when he took us all to Madame Taussauds and treats like that. But Fred won't have it.")

It was in August of 1910 that he said goodbye to Kathleen at Warrior Square Railway Station – with no one, according to Fred, being able to understand "the secrecy of his departure."

He was already dying and had, for quite some time, been spitting up blood every day – just like Frank Owen in the novel. He had just about managed to survive, financially, by sitting up in his sick-bed and inscribing the few coffin-plates he was able to obtain by way of work.

How, if this terrible prelude were true, could his death in Liverpool have come as such a horrifying surprise to Kathleen and the rest of his family?

For Fred, the prelude was true and Tressell's death confirmed it. The death also confirmed that Tressell's family, including Kathleen, were all callous and uncaring. Fred's outburst over the phone, which I quoted at the start of this memoir, shows that Fred never really believed Kathleen's account of her own distress. Obsession is a strange enough thing, but, in Fred's case, it was even stranger because his integrity compelled him to include her information but with an often subtle lack of endorsement. He even remarks (in his biography) that the missionary spirit was "strong" in the Tressell family, yet his obsession made him ignore the fact that the "bloody aunt" (who was herself blind in one eye) was pioneering a truly humanitarian school (one of the first in

Britain). All of the bloody family were working there devotedly, attending to the needs of the children – work which was often hard and couldn't offer very good pay. Inhumane people? Callous?

But I have to add, before we continue with Dr Davy's opinion about Tressell's death, that Kathleen had a lot to answer for. As Angela put it: "I sometimes think she's another Anastasia. Very much a dark horse. Poor old Fred!"

Kathleen was contradictory because she had her own reasons for being intimidated by the legend. And Fred did sometimes allow himself to be as fair to her as his bias itself would allow. Surely this does him credit, given that he couldn't understand her reasons for often being so evasive?

We are ourselves left with the fact that the prelude was not true and that the death did come as a shock to the family.

It was an unexpected death in every way. But that doesn't mean it wasn't on the cards. Tressell, for example, smoked incessantly – despite having what was called, in those days, a weak chest.

"It was all cough-cough-cough," Kathleen once told me, "early almost every morning, then nearly all day smoke-smoke-smoke. Aunt Addie couldn't stand the smoke. It was the last straw in one of their brother-and-sister rows. She cleared off because of the stink – not Socialism. Even if he hadn't died when he did, I suppose he might later on have died of lung-cancer."

Her father's reason for selling the furniture and moving into furnished lodgings in London Road was that he decided to give up most of his work and prepare for emigration. The lodgings were fully comfortable, and he and Kathleen had the run of the whole house – with Mrs Beaney, the wife of the landlord, doing the cooking. ("I was a rotten housekeeper," Kathleen also told me, "and Dad often said I was a wicked waster. He often said I would put him in the workhouse, but Fred got that all wrong. It was just a joke.")

As for the "secrecy of departure," Kathleen had written in the margin of the biography that her father had always kept his own business "to himself" and that there was "really no one else to consult" after he had made the arrangements for her to stay on with Aunt Jennie (at the School).

And let me just mention that before the lecture I had sent Kathleen a list of questions about that departure from the station in August. I don't think I risked quoting Kathleen's replies, but her father was wearing a smart tweed suit, straw hat and bow-tie. Mr Beaney had helped to crate up all he wanted to take (which went into the guard's van). I was not to learn more until, after the lecture, I went to see Kathleen (which merits a separate chapter), but one titbit I'll add here: he wasn't just in better health but had never been so prosperous locally. He had actually been earning more money than the notorious Misery.

More money than Misery? Good Heavens! But yes, he earned upwards of £3 per week basic.

In addition, he received incredibly handsome gratuities from time to time. For example, the elders of St Andrews Church were so impressed with the mural that they had a whip-round and got the vicar to present him with a testimonial and a five-pound note. (Fred gets the vicar's name slightly wrong, but Fred, although he minimises the occasion by saying Tressell argued against religion as he painted the mural, does have the integrity to mention this extra and huge sum of money.) Frankly, I feel green with envy to think the most I ever received, as a tip, was half-a-crown. (This was when I was working in the Normanhurst Hotel on the sea-front as a waiter – at the equivalent of 10 pence per hour – in 1953.) A five-pound note, I may perhaps need to remind some readers, was not the miserable polymer jam-pot label it is today. It was a rustling empyrean document, printed on white paper, which many people (including me in 1953) had never handled in all their lives, let alone received as a tip.

In returning to the subject of Tressell's "weak chest", I can only say that Kathleen wrote of it as meaning that her father often had a touch of bronchitis ("his usual bad cough"). Until she heard of it from Fred, the word "asthma" had never been mentioned by a doctor and "tuberculosis" never. He would only occasionally "go to the doctor."

In returning to the subject of Tressell's death, I shall now defer to Dr Davy (at that noisy party.)

"Assuming any patient to be in good health," he went on to say, rather too jovially, "an unexpected death in hospital is always going to look a bit like negligence – or even worse, ha ha!"

Quite sharply, I said: "How can any patient be described as being in good health if he or she has to go into hospital?"

He laughed at my pedantry and I remember he finished his drink before replying. "I mean, of course, a patient who is in good basic health except for a treatable ailment. Got it?"

I had reason to be a bit miffed with this very competent doctor. I respected him because he was a hero-doctor with the local lifeboat, but, consulting him a few weeks before with a bad sore throat, I was staggered to be told: "Don't worry, old chap. Take the pills and you'll soon recover. You're one of these chaps who send their wives out to work while you stay at home doing nothing. You're under no strain, you see. Big advantage, ha ha!"

I had croakily objected to this rashly unprofessional statement and he had hastily said: "Sorry, old chap. I'm sure your wife was only joking."

This joke of Angela's was becoming far too frequent with our friends and acquaintances and I was still brooding upon it. And Dr Davy saw again my slit-eyed gaze. He still saw the need to take care in trying to appease me. I am sure, therefore, that his medical opinion can be taken as reliable. I'll summarise it.

Although Kathleen was not qualified to judge her father's state of health during their shared life in Hastings, she did do a lot of nursing in Canada during her own life as an adult. Her retrospective testimony, as Dr Davy readily agreed, is worthy of belief. It would have been impossible for her not to have seen any signs of "coughing up blood," which Fred believed in as a daily symptom. Her father would not himself have put any member of his family at risk by ignoring such a symptom or keeping it a secret.

But he did suffer, on her testimony, from attacks of bronchitis and, unwisely continued to smoke but, in her words, always seemed able to "throw off" these attacks. He only coughed really badly in the afternoons if the Hastings weather was cold. As for "always being ill in bed," this impression could be due to his fondness for writing in bed – a penchant for many writers from Mark Twain to Lord Tennyson. (I even do it myself.)

"His health," as Kathleen wrote in the margin of Fred's biography, "had never been so good" as when she saw him off at the station, and she later said to me: "How could he have been half-starved, weak and ill and yet lift me off my feet in hugging me when we finally said goodbye? I was no slip of a girl. And why wasn't I half-starved as well?"

The shock of his death seems to have made it impossible for Kathleen to remember much of the circumstances that led up to it, to say nothing of the news of his burial which "seemed to happen in a flash." ("More on this shock in the next chapter.)

According to Dr Davy, going into hospital even in that early part of the twentieth century was not necessarily a fatal consequence. With good nursing, even "galloping consumption" as it used to be called (acute pneumonic phthisis) could be allayed if not remedied. But any sign of complication like bronchopneumonia, plus lowered resistance, should have been the signal for instant notification. The attendance of relatives (if the patient wants to see them) is always a vital aid to the renewal of resistance (both then as now).

Hence Dr Davy's conclusion: the hospital was negligent. Kathleen should have been sent the famous telegram before death, not after it.

"And I wouldn't mind betting," said Dr Davy, "that the death-certificate could have been a cover-up – possibly for an unattended choking-fit. Those boys could get away with anything. No one likely to complain, especially, "he added with a bit of grim cynicism before turning away, "if they're permitted to bung the dead patient into a common grave. Total anonymity assured."

This conversation with a brilliant but often indiscreet gossip of a doctor was a long time ago. I had no idea, when I was being cajoled into a lecture, that a pauper's grave was more legally known as a common grave. I had not heard of the term "common grave" until Dr Davy mentioned it, and Fred, I have to say, never used the legal term.

Angela, of course, had heard of the term when I asked her to get me up-to-date information about common-grave burial. (As I've mentioned before, she was six years older than I – and therefore better-versed in municipal customs.)

Not only did I discover, as time went on, that quite a few families had suffered the distress of mix-ups leading to such a burial – and, like the Tressell family, had painfully decided there was nothing they could do except keep quiet. I also discovered that the burials were often horrifying for being so brutishly careless.

Today, if you can stomach it, you can find the same information on the Internet.

Today, it is still a scandal that the dead – including babies among them – can be dumped like offal in half-filled pits slackly covered with a few boards. Foxes and rats are left to do their natural worst.

It would be a better memorial to Tressell, if I may say so as mildly as possible, if the Labour movement were to pioneer reform of common-grave burial. Meanwhile, it is hardly edifying that so many firms have sprouted who play upon the public fear of the common grave.

Too late in life, alas, I discovered that I had a grandfather who, before I was born, had been buried in a common grave. It must have been a closely-guarded secret, for I heard not one breath of it among my own often quarrelling relatives. Had I known of it when I knew Fred, it is just possible that I might have had less sidelong glances from him from time to time. Because I spoke with what he called a Received Accent, he sometimes seemed to suspect I might have noble blood in my veins.

Had I been able to tell him about the common grave in the family, plus the fact that I had a grandmother who had been a lady's maid – and who was descended from Welsh tinkers – my friendship with him might have survived the lecture.

I might also have been able to understand more immediately why Kathleen had the deeper problems I was to uncover in Bristol.

SIX

Tell Them I'm Dead

I

I nearly didn't go to Bristol.

To this day (even more extraordinarily), I can't remember any of my passing visits to that important city. I can only remember my emotions as I travelled back to Hastings after my interview with Kathleen. I shall describe those emotions, but, in advance, I need to reveal that I was inclined to see no point. I had already given the lecture. It had gone down reasonably well (except with Fred). I had a lot of work in hand. Kathleen had inexplicably postponed the interview, making it no longer urgent.

Going by the date of the recording I made of her (I wrote it on the label at the time), I am able to state that Astounding Friday (as I was to think of it later) as being on June 5th 1980. I can vaguely remember I had booked some sort of bed-and-breakfast place for the preceding day so as to be bang on time for the interview at St Monica's Home, Wing 2). Bristol is at quite a distance from Hastings, yet I simply cannot remember the long outward journey or the accommodation.

I can certainly remember the morning of my departure for Bristol very vividly indeed.

I rose early at half-past five. I made Angela a mug of tea and sat on her bed (to drink my own tea) while she, remaining in bed, yawningly but expertly began to advise me. (I can see her now!)

"You need," she said, "to relate to Kathleen in a special way that Fred can't. He can no more relate to her than a rhinoceros can relate to a tit-mouse. In other words, you need to relate to her personally but very delicately if you're to come back with a really good interview."

"And how," I said, in some petulance, "do you suggest I get around to being delicately personal?"

"By telling her," said Angela, becoming suddenly bright and alert, "all about the trouble I cause you."

From Angela, this was an unprecedented suggestion which I was too dim to grasp (especially at that time of the morning). I said: "You mean about your silly untrue jokes? Telling people I never do any work and so on?"

"Oh, but I never say things as bad as all that! Whatever makes you think so? I'm talking about an obvious fact and nothing more. Kathleen is very much a dark horse. Believe me, I can tell," and she added after a contented smile: "It takes one to know one."

"If you have so much in common with her," I said, as perplexed as a testy old stage-colonel, "come with me. You're certainly the one she dotes on. You come with me and I'll record your conversation. I'm sure it will be better than anything I can get out of her."

Ignoring this with one of her special chortles, Angela put down her mug of tea and jumped out of bed in the boisterous way she sometimes did. I do not exaggerate. She was behaving like a woman half her age. It was one of several sides to her personality, which many people of all ages found engaging – and including men, not all of them as old as Mr Pastry.

Opening the top drawer of her chest-of-drawers, she produced a favourite photograph of herself (mounted inside a folder and taken by Mr Pastry). Handing it to me, she got back into bed and resumed her tea (which she always alarmingly referred to as "corpse-reviver").

"Put that in your bag before you go," she said, "and give it to Kathleen. I don't want it back. It's one I often dish out. I haven't seen her for some time and it's just possible she can't quite remember what I look like. She's now a very old lady, don't forget."

"Perhaps," I said, "you ought to autograph it for the poor old thing."

Ignoring this sarcastic remark (as she did any remark she didn't wish to consider), Angela commanded me to make breakfast. As usual, I obeyed. Never in our marriage did we ever have a sit-down breakfast of the well-ordered kind we see in the movies, which was something I hankered after. My own childhood family never had a sit-down breakfast either. Furthermore, if I may be permitted another possibly irrelevant grievance, Angela couldn't cook. In that, it would seem, she had much in common with Kathleen while I, perhaps, and at least a little in common with Tressell for having wistful hopes of feminine domesticity. ("The only time we had nothing to eat," Kathleen had said, and even Fred mentions this in the biography, "was when I made something too inedible. We had to go out to a café.")

"Just do as I say," said Angela, hurrying my departure, "and everything will be all right. You confide in Kathleen and Kathleen will confide in you. I personally guarantee it. Don't go mucking things up in the same way as old Fred."

I became mutinous. I stated firmly: "I do not wish to do this interview. I don't see any necessity. The lecture is over and done with. I'll phone St Monica's and leave an apology for the old girl."

Angela was busy writing a note which she put into an envelope and licked down. This she shoved inside my meagre travel-bag and said: "You just open that envelope on your way back from Bristol. It will prove I'm right on at least one important point. I know exactly why Kathleen didn't go to see her father in hospital. Neither you nor Fred seem to understand why, but it's so obvious. Get the reason out of her then, afterwards, see if my theory is right. You will find that it is."

Angela was often annoyingly and intuitively so right that that I was really resentful in saying: "Have you any other theories you wish me to check?"

"Oh, but of course," she cheerfully gabbled, "but those I'm not sure of. For instance, it's obvious that Kathleen's father didn't go off to Liverpool to die in despair. So why did he go there? Remember that Kathleen sailed for Canada from Bristol. Significant point, little one! I think it possible that her mother was still alive. Living in Liverpool or near it. Tressell could have gone in search of reconciliation. You must ask Kathleen if she knows where her mother was buried. There would be a grave and the need for someone to pay for its upkeep. Unless, of course, it was another common-grave burial – in Cape Town! But that I rather doubt. I think Kathleen's mother very possibly ran away, off to America or somewhere, and, of course, she could have died there – if the story of her early death is true. On the other hand, she may have somehow ended up in Liverpool. I sure as eggs don't believe Kathleen's tale of being half-French and that she spoke fluent French as a child. She looks to me half-Boer, even in her photographs. Get going."

She virtually shoved me out of the door after thrusting my bag upon me, pausing only to lumber me with a pocket-sized volume of short-stories. (Oxford edition.) "Leave that with her, David, and tell her I want her to read Gissing's story called *A Daughter of the Lodge*. That daughter is very like Kathleen and even a bit like me! And just you remember what I've told you before. All women are at the mercy of their own bodies. You'll find Kathleen will agree. She'll know exactly what I mean. Jolly well ask her!"

II

Looking back after so many years, I am amazed by my past failure to see that Angela's behaviour was anything other than the sometimes amusing eccentricity of a "modern" career-woman.

But we all have this "failure" to perceive the odd things that happen to us, do we not?

We accept what happens to us, no matter how strange, simply because it happens in real life and not in a dream. We would only question oddities, I suggest, it they happen in dreams of the kind we call nonsensical the minute we wake up.

Sealing up a message to me and putting it in my bag? Giving me a photograph to give to Kathleen – and taken by Mr Pastry? Not all that strange? Perhaps not. But the consequences might strike you as being more than merely odd. (I'll mention here that Kathleen was already beginning to sign herself, in some of her letters to us, as "Kathleen the Mad." More than a little odd?)

Again, in contrast to her letters, she was not pleasant to meet in person when she opened the door to me in St Monica's Home (Wing 2).

The arrangement, as I understood it: to call at two o'clock after an early lunch taken by both parties separately. That's all I had in my mind. I don't remember how I found my way to her room and I cannot remember having had lunch myself. I had with me a bunch of flowers, but they must have been acquired by magic. I can't remember buying them.

"You're too early," was her only salutation when she opened her door.

I mumbled helpless apologies and presented the flowers. She accepted them without a word and let me enter the room and sit down. She gave my relatively humble recording-equipment a critical glance, perhaps having become blasé after giving so many interviews. Perhaps she had expected me to turn up with a film-crew? For the technically minded: all I had brought along (slung around my neck in its black container) was the little Phillips portable recorder, popular in those days for being cheap, light in weight and of tolerable fidelity to those with expertise. I fancied I had this expertise. Two voices are easy to balance, even with the cheapest microphone. To impress Kathleen with my expertise, I had sent her a copy of my booklet *Tape Recording Local History*. (She didn't read it but "liked the cover.")

In itself, interviewing held no terrors for me. I had recorded quite a few voices after 1962, but recording Lady Bracknell in 1980 was a prospect I found myself earnestly wishing to avoid.

"I haven't even had time," said Lady Bracknell, "to put my new frock on."

There it was, the new frock – hanging on the wall from a dress-hanger and looking all the more frightening for being disembodied. It was blue with white spots and had a severe white collar.

"You don't really need to worry about what you look like," I said, washing my hands with invisible soap and water. "It's purely audio. But, if you'd prefer it, I can go away now – and come back a bit later," (which, frankly, I had no intention of doing once I got away).

"Now that you're here," this difficult old lady said, "we might as well get on with it. Perhaps you might do a little better this time. Previous efforts have not been good, have they?"

There was an instant transformation the moment I switched on the tape-recorder.

To use Angela's description, the "sweetie-sweet" act took over. No one could ever believe, let me say, that Kathleen could be so ghastly if the sweetie-sweet act was all they had ever experienced.

As a standard-type interview, it was actually quite good and I'll put it on the Internet if enough people are interested. I was as tactful and as "safe" as possible and Kathleen replied dutifully, but it was not in any way inspiringly impromptu. Almost everything she said had been said, word-for-word, in reply to other people at other times (and even to me).

One possible difference. To my surprise, she rather coldly said that her aunt (Jennie) and her companion Louise Osbourne "were probably lesbian" and had slept in the same bed. I thought it to be a silly remark and that she was trying to seem modern and sophisticated. In other conversations, I had already heard her using popularised words from psycho-analysis, such as "complex" and "empathy" which had been the talk of the twenties. Although I was in no way an expert in this field of study, I did at least know the terms and knew that Kathleen had no real knowledge of their meaning. I have to say it: to judge from that recording and her topics of conversation generally, she had become trivial. I had gone from being scared to being bored.

I had no idea that we could enter into any sort of deeper discussion about her father.

We got to the end of the cassette and I was about to pack up and leave. I had no intention of "getting personal" about myself or allowing the absent Angela to obtrude as a form of subject-matter. I had forgotten all about Mr Pastry's photograph of her and her sealed envelope – and also the book with the story about the daughter of the lodge. These items were in my bag on the floor beside my chair.

I was still in a state of bewilderment, although, as I have said, bored.

Why had she been so unpleasant when she opened the door?

It was to be quite some time, back in Hastings, before the reason dawned upon me. Having no wish to leave any reader in so equal a bewildered state, I am going to give her reason before I write about the rest of that surprising afternoon.

The reason centred upon the conspiracy hatched by the three Tressells earlier on. First, they had wanted me to become a joint-author, with Fred. The idea which they had discussed with Angela beforehand (and had her blessing) was that this "would tone Fred down."

I had been unco-operative. The biography was duly published. The conspirators then changed tack.

The next idea, which was reasonably successful, was to get me to deliver a corrective lecture. You will remember that I was told, before the lecture, that Kathleen would grant me an audience to assist my preparation. I was then left in my first stage of bewilderment. There was a seemingly pointless change of schedule. I was to be granted audience after the lecture instead of before it. Here's why.

What had happened was that Kathleen had decided not to attend the lecture but to leave it to Joan and Reginald to judge its success. She would then grant me the audience, highly private and giving me enough new material for a new and rival biography. This would have been impossible for me even if I had the time to write it. It was also a ridiculous idea, in my view; but I had vaguely got wind of it and had, equally vaguely, made a light-hearted reference to my disinclination in a letter to Kathleen. I had then forgotten about this letter and not realised how much it had annoyed her. Hence the ungracious way she received me.

Have you got all that?

Now for what happened next. It was what novelists call a pivotal moment. She offered me coffee. She tittered a little. This put me more at ease and I accepted. She poured it out from a Thermos-jug and said: "Have you listened to any of the tapes I made with Fred?"

"No," I had to tell her. (And, to this day, I have never wished to listen to them. For me, the very thought is delicately unbearable.)

Still inclined to titter, Kathleen said: "Has your wife listened to any of those tapes?"

"Not as far as I know."

Although not reverting to Lady Bracknell, Kathleen at this point suddenly became less tittery and more incisive. She said: "The invitation for this visit was for both of you. It was your wife I was looking forward to seeing. Why isn't she with you?"

"She just couldn't make it, I'm afraid, but she sends her

apologies and her kind regards." (This was a bit of a white lie, but I was fairly used to telling white lies on Angela's behalf.)

"I especially wanted to see her," said Kathleen. "In my opinion, she and I have a lot in common. Is her own father still alive?"

"I'm sorry to say he isn't. Died a few years ago.

"In the workhouse, by any chance?"

"Actually," I said, hoping this might in some way comfort Kathleen, "he did crack a joke about that. So do other local people if they have to go into that hospital," (St Helen's, Frederick Road) "because it used to be part of the workhouse in your time in Hastings. So people do often speak of ending up in the workhouse. It's just a local historical joke."

"And Fred, of course, doesn't mention THAT in his biography! He just goes on repeating that Dad died in the workhouse when he did not. DID NOT"

I could see a glistening of Kathleen's eyes and I got up and hastily offered to pour her another coffee. (Someone had evidently left two Thermos jugs with us – one with hot milk in it and the other the coffee.) An old lady in tears? Unbearable.

Recovering slightly, Kathleen tried to make a little tittering joke of her own. But with a bit of a sting in it. She said: "When your wife's father was dying in the Hastings workhouse, I don't suppose she was accused of not bothering to go and see him?"

"Actually," I said, and only because it was the truth, "Angela never went to see him in hospital. She left all the visiting to her mother and me. Even when he was actually dying."

Frown from Kathleen: "And I don't suppose you even thought of asking why! And why call her Angela?"

"It's just a joke-name," I said, feeling idiotic at having let it slip. "Angela of the Upper Fifth. Private nick-name. Never used in public."

Kathleen interrupted my explanation with a sudden and sharper sting in her voice.

"David, would you like to know WHY I didn't go to see my father in hospital?"

Feeling even more idiotic, I said: "Only if you want to tell me."

"David, this is something I did try to tell Fred. He couldn't understand. I was in love. Or rather," said Kathleen, correcting herself in a quite bitter tone, "I thought I was in love. And I thought I was in love because, David, I wanted to be in love. I was so stupidly wrapped up in myself I couldn't think of anything else. I was too young to know what I was doing. I never thought anything could be really wrong with my father."

She nearly broke down on those last few words and I felt very guilty at having upset her. What could I do? Change the subject. That's it – change the subject.

"By the way," I said, after gently daring to pat her inert hand, "Angela wants me to give you a book, which I've brought with me … and a rather nice colour-photograph of herself."

I unzipped my travel-bag and breezily delved inside for the book and the photograph. I had completely forgotten about the sealed envelope, and, of course, that's what I came across first. Although I was under orders not to open it until "on the way back," I naughtily opened it. A short note on blue Basildon Bond.

It read: "The reason why K never went to see her father in hospital was because she was in love. Has she told you or have you worked it out for yourself? I'm sure she felt exactly as I felt in 1947 when I fell for that boy-friend from hell. I bet she's had one as well. Like me, too young to know what she was doing. Destroy this."

I destroyed the note, but only the other day – in other words, in 2017. (I rediscovered it after having forgotten I'd kept it for 37 years.)

To return to 1980: I put the note in the inside-pocket of my jacket. I put the book containing the Gissing short-story on the table and I offered the photograph to Kathleen.

She was sunk in thought, gazing distantly, and I had to nudge her (as it were) by saying: "Kathleen, the photograph …"

I felt stunned, not by the reference to the boy-friend from

hell (Angela often spoke acidly about him) but by the accuracy of Angela's prediction of having been in love. I was so stunned I hardly noticed the coincidental bit "too young to know what she was doing." I was thinking: "If old Angela is as accurate as this, she could be right about Liverpool."

Kathleen not only took the photograph but sat looking at it through a horn-rimmed magnifying-glass.

May I remind you that no one, at this time, knew that Tressell had ever lived in Liverpool; and, according to some researchers, had been imprisoned there for theft. It was also not yet known that Tressell, in Africa, had divorced his wife for adultery and had been granted sole custody of the child. I have not yet checked these later stories. There is no reason to think they might in any way be untrue or inaccurate. I'll only say that Fred had dissected so many convincing red herrings that no alternative variation would surprise me. It can only be said with certainty that Kathleen knew nothing of the term of imprisonment. And she knew almost nothing about her mother. She didn't even know her mother's real name (Elizabeth) until Fred himself found it out and was thus able to tell her of it in 1967. (And as he tells us in the biography.)

Angela, I should also add, was intuitively right if the imprisonment-story is true. She had said to me, a few weeks before the lecture: "I wonder what Fred would feel if Tressell turns out to be rather like Gissing? These details are always exaggerated, but Gissing did go to prison for stealing money from his fellow-students. But even Gissing didn't starve as much as his admirers make out. He used to give English lessons. And the story about marrying a prostitute is probably another exaggeration. It would break Fred's heart if anything like that is ever said of Tressell."

I've no wish to sound too twee and fastidious, but, after that last remark by Angela, my reluctance to delve too deeply for "the truth" had become a feeling of acute anxiety.

What sort of a rotter would wish to break Fred Ball's heart?

Worse still, now that I was in Bristol, Angela's remark was adding very drastically to my personal mystification.

What on earth, I was asking myself, am I doing? Why am I even bothering to extend this hitherto mostly abortive interview?

I think I should give you a bit of an answer in advance. Only half-knowing it at the time, I was looking for what I call the ultimate Tressellian value. It was eluding me in the way a rare plant might elude a fanatical botanist on a very high cliff. Lying flat on his stomach, he would be reaching down to a perilous ledge. The specimen would be growing there, dangerously beyond his finger-tips. But it wasn't altogether identifiable – and perhaps wasn't worth the risk of reaching for.

At this stage of this memoir, that's all I can say about my reasons for going to Bristol.

I can only add that I would never have found the ultimate value had I not gone.

III

"I think," announced Kathleen, still studying the photograph, "that Angela is a better name for your wife than her real name."

Henceforth, when referring to Angela, Kathleen was to emphasise the name in a way that Angela herself would have thought intrusively familiar.

"And David," said Kathleen, with a giggle, "this is a really charming photograph. When did you take it? Was it on some sort of ramble?"

"Not one of mine," I curtly said. "It was taken by that curator-chap who stepped in to save the mural. He's retired now. I don't even know where it was taken or when. She wants you to have it, that's all."

"So how old was Angela when the curate took this nice lovely photograph?"

"Curator," I corrected her, and irritably. "You've called him a curate before. He's a parish-clerk, whatever that is, but not a curate. She was about 45 when that was taken, I suppose."

"Oh but David," said Kathleen, "she looks half that age! How does she do it?"

"According to the doctor, she has a slightly over-active thyroid. That's the explanation, she thinks. It's why she refuses to have anything done."

"Yes, David, I've noticed she does have a slight bulgy throat sometimes. But that surely can't be the whole explanation. Oh, she looks so happy!"

"The whole explanation," I said and rather sarcastically, "is probably due to the fact that she spends a lot on herself. Also, of course, she refuses to believe she can grow old. That probably helps. But I am not here, if I may say so, to talk about Angela. I never even think about her age."

Kathleen was not the first to be impressed by Angela's photogenic qualities, but she was perhaps the most persistent among women. Mischievously, she said: "And did you have a Quaker wedding? What was it like? Was it in Hastings? Did a lot of Quakers attend in funny black hats? Like that picture of a Quaker on a Quaker Oats packet?"

"Allow me to inform you," I pompously said, "that Quakers have nothing to do with Quaker Oats. Furthermore, we were married in the local registry-office in Wellington Square. And it was as sparsely attended," I added, "as a pauper's funeral."

The word "clanger" was often used in those days to describe something one says which is so appalling one can't believe oneself for having said it. I had dropped many a clanger in my naïve youth, but at 49? At a relatively mature age? I cannot describe my horror and my bewilderment. Why had I said such a terrible thing? And to Tressell's daughter of all people?

If you consider the clanger to be strange (as you should, in my opinion,) then the effect of it upon Kathleen was just as strange.

Her face straightened and she simply looked away. After a

moment, she slowly nodded to herself. It was a slow, up-and-down form of nod, which I crassly assumed to be a symptom of senility. (She was 88 at the time of this interview.)

"David," she dreamily said, "I have very happy memories of Wellington Square. It wasn't very far from Milward Road. All sorts of gatherings on the grass in the middle. Had picnics there. I knew the Cruttendens of course ..."

"How very interesting," I cried, eager to develop this tangent. (I was hoping it would serve to obliterate my clanger.) "Of course," I babbled on, "it's of great significance to Angela. She had a bit of a row with her parents and left home – and got a lodging just at the top of the Square, where, as it happens, she was living when I first met her. Her landlady was called Miss Dunk."

"A quarrel?" asked Kathleen. "What about?"

"Oh, just some boy-friend her parents didn't approve of," and this information of mine led to Kathleen revealing the quarrel (which I've already mentioned) which Kathleen had with her father.

With a crass lack of tact (the quarrel having been about Kathleen's wish to go on the amateur stage,) I breezily said: "Oh, Angela had no trouble on that score! Her parents encouraged her zeal for theatricals," and I rattled off her triumphs.

Kathleen began to look so wistful that I hastily changed the subject back to the Square.

"And, of course, Angela went to a little private school in Wellington Square," and I condescendingly added: "Rather pretentiously called Wellington College. It's a hotel now. And guess what. I once ran a woodwork business and one day I was in that hotel, putting up notice- boards – and without knowing it was Angela's old school! How's that for a funny coincidence?"

"And how's this," said Kathleen, quietly and calmly, "for an even funnier one? I was very nearly sent to that same school."

Normally, I have to say, I would agree with any reader who might think this detail to be too trivial to be mentioned. But for me, at the time, this was a very neat little put-down.

In the parlance of that time, I could also be described as having just been up-staged. It was a surprise, but I felt like applauding. Although I have never wanted to be an actor, I have always been sympathetic to actors and their problems. (I had founded a drama-recording group principally to help them.) The point I'm making here is that Kathleen had just confirmed what I had discovered some ten years before – namely, that she was a born actress and was still capable of putting on a well-controlled act.

"I would like to have gone to Wellington College," she went on, looking openly delighted by my surprised expression, "but I couldn't be taken in as a boarder. So I was sent away …"

Like many grown-ups who have been "sent away" to boarding schools, we exchanged a few horror-stories which I agree are not likely to interest readers who were educated more humanely. I'll only make two points which are relevant to this memoir. First, when damage is done by being "sent away" at too young an age, it remains done. That was as true for Kathleen as it was for me – and for many others of our respective generations.

The second point (which may well escape many adherents to the Tressell legend) was that fees were not as astronomical as they are today. Even my own school, in 1942, charged my father only £52 per year. Tressell, we can be sure, was charged less and was obviously able to afford it. Fred, who sometimes seemed to think I'd been sent to Eton College, had been irked to find that Kathleen had partly experienced the same "privileged" education.

In not pursuing the truth about it with any sympathy, he missed some further details about Kathleen. I am now publishing them here for the first time, but have to say that without Angela's photograph they might never have come to light.

Kathleen had laid aside her magnifier but was intermittently gazing at the photograph as if looking at herself in a mirror. She said: "Did Angela like the photo of me I sent her – and of course to you," she charitably added.

"Both of us," I said, "were most impressed," and, indeed,

we were. But there was something I didn't mention. Kathleen had written on the back: "The nitwit who sold the MS." Angela had studied those words far longer than she had studied the photograph. Angela had said: "This innocent-looking girl who sold the MS" (manuscript) "was no nitwit. She knew what she was doing. And she hasn't altered, you can bet your best Quaker Oats hat."

The photograph of Kathleen, as I sincerely said, was impressive. She had adopted a calmly "intellectual" pose with an open book on the table before her. She also looked attractively strong-willed and capable. In that photograph, she had looked to me like Gissing's heroine in *A Daughter of the Lodge*. But it just so happened that I thought another photograph of her to be somehow more special.

I delved into my travel-bag for my copy of Fred's *One of the Damned* where the photograph is reproduced. (You will find it facing page 43 in the 1973 Weidenfeld and Nicolson hardback, but facing page 75 in the 1979 paperback published by Lawrence and Wishart.)

The caption states the date as August 1913.

Jokingly, I said: "I've brought old Fred's book with me. I thought you might like to write 'bosh' in the margin at one or two other points."

She laughed happily at this bit of teasing. (The book had already been annotated with the help of the other two Tressells.) But, foolishly, I extended the teasing. I knew the photograph was not of Kathleen dressed as a servant-girl, yet I pretended to think so.

"I particularly like," I said, "this picture of you in servant-girl garb. I think the mob-cap is most becoming. But this lovely dark tress dropping down from your shoulder strikes me as a little too enticing for work with a dustpan and brush. Were you trying the hook the son of the house?"

I was trying to tell her that she looked simply stunning in that photograph. Why couldn't I have simply said that? Instead, I had unleashed a not and furious stare.

"You will pardon me, Mr Quaker Haines," she said, and with an amazing colour on her cheeks, "but, like Mr Ball, you have got that photo all wrong. For one thing, it was not taken in 1913. I was still at school. It was more 1909 or possibly 1910. But Mr Ball thinks he knows best – as he does about everything."

Feebly apologising but staggered by this fury, I said: "Very sorry. Just a joke. I'll alter the date," and I did so there and then.

"We used to play tennis sometimes dressed like that," she said, "but it was possibly for some senior school occasion. Are you so stupid you can't see my school-satchel?"

I looked for what she called a satchel and, again, was stupid enough to anger her still more – this time with a contradiction.

"I can't see any sign of a satchel. There isn't one."

"Then what," she said, turning freezingly contemptuous, "is in my hand?"

"It looks more like a suitcase to me," I said, making things worse for myself. "A small suitcase, but definitely a suitcase and not what I would call a satchel. A satchel has a shoulder-strap ..."

My voice petered out.

"It had a shoulder-strap," she gratingly said, "but I had unclipped it. It could be carried like a small suitcase. It also fitted to the carrier on the back of my bicycle. It also had on it my initials – which my father himself had painted so as to prevent mistakes in the cloak-room."

Kathleen now came out without something, which, for me, was an extraordinary revelation.

"That's why I was called Kenny at school."

"Kenny?" This was brand-new information.

"Because of my initials on the satchell – K.E.N."

"Those were your initials? What did they stand for?"

"Kathleen Elizabeth Noonan," she snapped. "What else could they stand for?"

To this day, not many people seem to know that Kathleen had the additional name Elizabeth. (It is not recorded in the references to her as Tressell's daughter, as far as I know.)

Cautiously, I said: "So you were named after your mother?"

"What are you driving at? My mother was French and she died of typhoid when I was three. I've told you that before. So what are you driving at?"

"Since your mother's name has turned out to be Elizabeth," I said, even more cautiously, "it seems likely that you were named after her."

With a slight toss of her head, Kathleen changed the subject in a clever, schoolgirlish sort of way. (Half-changed the subject, in other words.) She said: "One of my friends went to Wellington College, but both she and I went to the PT-School eventually. Up on The Ridge. 1907."

She was referring to the Pupil-Teacher School (later the High School.) So I said: "I can get Angela to check if she's still living in Hastings. Although Wellington College has long gone, the old former pupils still have reunions – in what is now the hotel. Angela might even know your friend. Shall I get her to look into all this?"

"You can if you wish," was the ungracious reply. "We were hoping to become teachers."

"What was the name of your friend?"

"I can't remember and she's probably dead."

I now compounded all my blunders. Thinking I had struck gold and might strike more, I got up from my chair to get at my tape-recorder. Mad enough to think I could switch on without Kathleen noticing, I was fumblingly crouched over it. All I succeeded in doing was to drop the cassette.

"What," she said, sitting bolt upright, "do you think you're doing?"

"I just thought we ought to do a bit more recording …"

"You've already got a recording. You don't need another and

I don't even know why you've got that. You've given your lecture. And you've made something else very clear, haven't you?"

"I don't know what you mean."

"Of course you do!"

She was a less weighty-looking woman at this time than when I first met her, and I would say was actually looking fitter despite being so much older. She quite sprang out of her chair. I thought she was about to shake me by the arm, as she perhaps did with her charges when she was a nursery-governess in London. (This was something my mother's live-in home-help used to do to me when I was very small, and I've never got over it.)

I don't mind admitting that I shrank back, but my fears of assault on those grounds were groundless. She had sprung up to rummage somewhere, panting so much that I had a new fear — that she might have a stroke. This fear, too, was groundless. She merely produced a letter of mine, dated April 8th 1980. Therefore recent. (I know the date because I have the carbon-copy of this ingratiating letter in front of me right now.)

Standing as if she were on a stage, Kathleen read out just one paragraph.

> About this business of writing a biography of your Pa. I've decided I can't do it because of the difficulties with publishers. Also, I am wondering if it's the right thing to do. I don't want to hurt anyone's feelings, which includes Fred Ball.

Grimly folding up the letter, she sat down to berate me. I don't exaggerate. Various women have berated me over the years, but this example was bad enough to convince me that quarrels in the Tressell household must have been worse than any sentimental admirers could imagine. I won't include everything Kathleen said, but here is an edited version. Who would have thought one little paragraph could so suddenly give rise to such a squall?

"Mr Haines, you have repeatedly betrayed me right from the start. Over and over again, you have refused to write a biography that could put things right. Even in this letter you harp on about your silly objections."

"I just wanted," I feebly said, "to prevent any further misunderstanding."

"So why come here – after the lecture and without your wife – to ask questions which have no further point? Why are you getting me to say things which I never meant to tell you? Why sneakily try to tape them?"

Since I didn't know my deeper reasons for coming to Bristol, my reply sounded a lot worse that feeble – it sounded unconvincing.

"I sort of thought," I said, not quite cowering in my chair (but not far from it,) "that something ought to be recorded for posterity."

"Posterity," she rapped out, "can look after itself. I still want to know why you're really here."

This demanding statement was so fierce that it stimulated the beginnings of an explanation, albeit just as feeble-sounding.

"If I may put it this way," I said, "I'm sort of looking for one important truth about, er, your father's values. What might be called, er, Tressellian values. I sort of feel there has to be one ultimate value, which can have the greatest significance for all of us. I, er …"

My voice faltered away, but Kathleen pounced vociferously.

"What rubbish are you spouting now? There is only one ultimate value which you, Mr Haines, need to look for. Which we all need to look for. And that's the teaching of our Lord Jesus Christ. Do you agree to that or not?"

She had brought up this subject before, in Hastings, but I couldn't remember when and my struggles to recall the occasion increased her anger.

"Tell me this once and for all! Answer me! Are you a communist? Is that it? You seek to crush all Christianity? As in Russia?"

"Certainly not," I said, but still as weak as water. "One of your father's inferred but great values is the value generally known as respect. Both for religion and, of course, democratic political systems. Provided," I found the audacity to add, "they don't become hateful and cruel alternatives."

"Don't you dare preach to me," said Kathleen, almost jumping out of her chair again. "You've even betrayed your own religion. My father had a friend who was a Quaker. Very nice man, not like you and Fred Ball. I've just remembered that."

"How interesting," I said, in all sincerity. "Remember his name, can you? Worth checking."

"Worth checking? Why? You think I'm telling lies? That's pretty rich, coming from someone like you – a deserter from the Army."

This accusation was the most incredible and the nastiest of surprises so far. I honestly thought I had mis-heard.

"A deserter from the Army?" I repeated this as if I had just been coshed over the head.

"According to Angela," said Kathleen, again with a special emphasis, "you did very little National Service. You were court-martialled and chucked out within a matter of months."

Although stunned, I treated this accusation light-heartedly (or tried to), I said: "But surely it was for cheating at cards, wasn't it? I don't think you've got that particular story quite right."

"It was for desertion," said Kathleen, firmly and contemptuously. "You told all sorts of lies at the court-martial. You pretended your grandmother had died. She hadn't, had she? You simply ran away."

I stood up.

"For your information, madam, the reason for my discharge – and I can prove it – is as follows. I quote. Ceasing to fulfil Army physical requirements."

There was no court-martial.

I picked up the coffee-tray. I added: "I think I'd better go in search of more coffee. We can then perhaps bring this unpleasant encounter to a reasonably amicable end."

VI

I had no idea of where to go with the tray and the two Thermos jugs. Setting off from Kathleen's door, I was in a state of mind I can only partly describe.

I still have no memory of where I wandered in that building or for how long. Had it not been for my having left my travel-bag and the recorder with Kathleen, I would have dumped that tray and cleared off. I was furious with Angela and Kathleen, the one for telling this absurd story and the other for believing it.

"Bloody women," I must admit to having muttered, and I think I was sitting down in some corridor or other with the tray chattering on my petulant knees. (I seem to recall someone passing me but looking at me with a total lack of curiosity.)

Whether anyone else approves of this or not, I am now going to recount a memory which was flooding my mind. It was one of the most vivid experiences of my life. I started to recall it the moment I left Kathleen's door. Although I had no knowledge of Tressellian values at the time, this experience had led me to make a decision which, in my opinion, was compatible with them. I was never a profound thinker. It was my feelings which had decided me, but I had only been 13 at the time and still at boarding-school.

A kind and gentle Quaker teacher had taken a group of us for a cross-country walk (popularly known as a pig-drive). He was genuinely loved and respected (unlike some of our teachers) and there was no doubting his courage. He had been an ambulance-driver, often under fire, in the 1914 war. We had arrived at a secluded ford on a country road not far from our boarding-school.

It was a favourite destination, especially to go there with a girl-friend (unusually, for those days, our school was co-educational).

You could paddle there or chuck stones in to splash the girls sitting on the side-walk bridge.

We all sat down in the long grass of a nearby space to watch a group of American soldiers. They were enjoying a break from driving their lorries to some secret place – mustering for D-Day.

To amuse us and themselves, they began driving their lorries to-and-fro through the ford. It was all great fun. The splashes were excitingly magnificent.

But, as most of the members of the pig-drive began to realise, these soldiers could soon be dead. This thought seemed evident in the face of a much older sergeant who stood watching them indulgently. The soldiers under his command could only have been five or six years older than ourselves. The sergeant was leaning against the rail on the side-walk bridge and giving a little shrug at the biggest splashes.

"Murderers! Murderers in uniform!"

To the amazement of some of us at least, these were the words our teacher suddenly started to shout. He beckoned to those of us dodge-daring the splashes, and I can still remember the sadness of the sergeant's smile as he turned to look in the direction of the shouts. And his final little shrug.

Obediently and with some of us rather damp, we walked back to school without saying anything. But we had our thoughts. I, for one, realised then that even the best of people can be fanatical and, in being fanatical, unkind and stupidly unjust.

It was this incident which decided me, when I was 18, to raise no objection to National Service.

In returning to Kathleen's room with the tray, I very probably returned with the two Thermos jugs unreplenished. I cannot recall anyone re-filling them for me or washing the cups. I faintly remember a wash-room or laundry but no kitchen or refectory. Not that this was to matter very much. Neither of us, as I recall, seemed to want any more coffee. But my idiotic excursion with the tray was not, I think, a waste of time. I had managed to restrain my anger but I was determined not to put up with any more old buck.

I had obviously been away for some time because, when she opened the door to me, Kathleen had changed into the new dress (the one previously hanging on the wall).

"Oh, David – I am sorry! I apologise. I must have got hold of the wrong end of the stick – about the Army, I mean."

"No further need to discuss it," I briskly said.

"Oh, but there is! Are you a pacifist now?"

"I've always been one," I said, "but, I hope, with common-sense reservations. Any man who bashes me gets bashed back."

I rather rudely sat down but I was otherwise being careful not to offend her. Had I not known how "difficult" she could be, her manner from now on was so charming I would have been completely bowled over. I could actually see a youthful likeness in her face to her own early photographs. It was like seeing her youth pouring back into her like fresh spring water filling a glass. She said: "Surely you were very unhappy to be in the Army?"

"I was not. I even went on a walking-tour to get myself fit and ready. To Ireland. I was very politely discharged because I revealed that I'd been to a Quaker school. Not officer-material."

"To Ireland? Oh, how wonderful! I've always wanted to go to Ireland. Have you been to Dublin?"

"I have, yes. I was to see children there, running about in rags and bare feet. Hansom-cabs, too. It was like stepping back in time to 1900."

I took Fred's book *One of the Damned* from my bag and added: "Let's get back to the point in the here and now. I'd like to clear up one or two inconsistencies in your testimony. But I am no longer a Quaker. Get that straight. No more jokes, please."

Kathleen instantly sat down to say: "David, I've done nursing for over 20 years. I want to help you. I've realised your wife is rather strange."

"You can say that again," I disloyally muttered.

"Seriously, David, there's something wrong in the way she talks about you. I honestly think she's got a complex. I think she ought to see a psychoanalyst. Fred, of course, doesn't believe in it. Did you notice what he wrote in his silly preface?"

Kathleen was referring to the preface where Fred makes a comment about people "intruding between a man and his work with amateur psycho-analysis." Was this a dig at Kathleen? Or perhaps me? But I think Fred had a point. And I don't want to offend any followers of Freud if they happen to be Tressell enthusiasts when I hereby say Freud had struck me as pessimistic and depressing. I had given up on psychoanalysis, but I knew that lots of people were utterly devoted to Freud. (Years later I was to see a young woman storm out of a discussion where I, among others, had ventured to criticise. I never saw or was able to speak to her again.) I don't think Kathleen had any studious knowledge of Freud, but, given as she was to bits of talk about "complexes" and so on, I didn't want to risk our friendship any further.

Forcing myself to smile cosily, I intensely said: "Let's just put all that stuff to one side, shall we? We really do need to stick to the point if we're to get anything of value out of all the confusion."

Kathleen was now doing her best to extend an olive-branch and was grinning happily. This little tiff had seemed to do her good.

Because she was now being charmingly well-behaved, I decided to begin a deeper exploration of the legend with a simple (and, I thought, safe) little mystery. It was a harmless absurdity, which had puzzled several experienced writers. Fred, in his biography, contended that Tressell "had a tin box made" for sending out his manuscript to publishers. This would have been an amateurish thing to do because it would have added prohibitively to the postal weight. A cardboard box, perhaps; but a tin box? And an entire, hand-written manuscript?

To my surprise, Kathleen went all jittery. She said, almost

angrily: "I am not going to talk about the manuscript. Get that clear, David."

"All I'm asking about," I said, "is the tin box Fred mentions. Where did Fred get this story from?"

"And I'm telling you," she said, pretty much through clenched teeth, "that I don't want to talk about the manuscript."

I hastily dropped the subject of the tin box.

V

"Oh, tell them I'm dead!"

This angry instruction to her husband, Paul, was Kathleen's additional contribution to the misleading Tressell legend. Her marriage in Canada had "gone wrong" in a fashion which should, I think, remain mostly private. (Fred gives as many details as he could in his biography and I won't repeat them, except where there is a major misinterpretation.) She was in the distressing situation where she was deserting her husband and absconding with their baby daughter. Her husband, who was a first cousin, had distressingly asked: "What shall I tell the family?"

We now know the answer she gave him, but Fred either ignored or hadn't seen the cold flash of venom she displayed (to me) in repeating it.

In this part of my interview with her, she became quite recklessly informative now the cat was more out of the bag. She even giggled at various moments, but, here and there, would have sudden misgivings and say: "I hope you're not secretly recording all this?"

"No," I would each time say.

"You're sure? I hope I can trust you."

"You can trust me, my dear Miss Noonan."

Despite my tolerant bonhomie, I was really rather shocked by how coldly callous she was at certain moments towards her own relatives. But, as part of the process as it were, she would soften and express contrition. Alice, for example, her other cousin: Kathleen had been jealous of the attention her father had given her (as she admitted,) but, in her next breath said: "I shudder to think of Fred badgering that poor blind woman."

Fred was always to express annoyance with Alice, his first and major informant. It says something for Fred's egocentricity that I, like many others, didn't know this major informant had been blind from birth. Fred simply ignored the fact in complaining about her lack of co-operation. It wasn't until after my lecture that Joan revealed to me that Alice had been blind and had talents of no interest to Fred whatsoever. Angela, incidentally, was highly scornful of Fred when I first told her of Alice. ("The galumphing idiot should have let me go and see her!") Alice, in fact, didn't die until 1962. A more tactful researcher than Fred could, I'm sure, have extracted the information she withheld – namely, that Kathleen and her child had not been killed in a motor-car accident.

That, of course, had long been the cover-story given out by husband Paul, but, inevitably, the bloody aunts and various other parties (such as the RTPs first publisher) all learnt the truth. I do feel sorry for Fred for being kept in the dark, but he was too proprietorial for his own good. Even in the biography, he doesn't consider that Alice was protecting the family's privacy from the "shame" of a pauper's burial. Nor does he consider that Mr Richards, the publisher, had been hoodwinked by Kathleen and was, perforce, obliged to protect the publicity. The legend she had set in train was already growing like a snowball running away downhill. A working-class novel written by a builder's labourer! By Jove!

It isn't even true that Tressell was in the building-trade, as depicted in the cover-illustration to the popular 1927 edition (of the Pope Abridgement). It shows builders precariously shifting girders in a huge building under construction. Tressell was solely a sign-writer and decorator. Meanwhile, Kathleen and her daughter were caught up in this tangle of shame about the burial, the family's illegitimacy and the publisher's commercial interests.

It wasn't even true (as wrongly reported at the time) that Kathleen's "return from the dead" was in 1967 (when she gave that talk at the Railway Club.) She had been to Hastings, unknown to us all, twice before her dramatic visit in 1967. She had come to settle financial matters with the family she had left behind when she went off to Canada. She was even to hint to me that her husband somehow cheated her out of the deed to a small but valuable bit of land owned by her father in South Africa. ("I signed something I shouldn't have signed.")

The reason I have said, earlier in this memoir, that Fred was biased but not a bigot is that he undoubtedly filtered everything through a closely-woven net of bias. But, had Fred been a bigot, he would have filtered everything through a net with a far tighter mesh. He allows stuff through which, if you read between the lines without bias yourself, will show you gleams of truth. Rather like scratching the wall in that chancel and finding Tressell's mural gleaming beneath? Perhaps that's too mixed a metaphor, but, had Fred been a bigot, he would never have mentioned (for example) the informant who told him that Tressell would "walk away" from a job if he didn't like it. A workman who is in a position to "walk away" from a job is hardly likely to be starving. A bigot is always totally ruthless about facts which don't suit his case. Fred obviously didn't like having to include facts which didn't suit his case. But he included them if he found them. That's partly why, in my opinion, his biography of Tressell is among the great biographies. ("All this," he remarks about certain awkward facts and perhaps rather sadly, "seems a far cry from my poverty-struck decorator.")

Fred's problem as a biographer, put simply, was that he was too biased to ask someone like Kathleen the right questions ... and in the right way. But please note. Even when one is as "impartial" as possible with someone as guilt-ridden as Kathleen, it is not easy to ask the right questions at the right time (to say nothing of the right way). In this second part of this encounter (a better name for it than "interview"), Kathleen was as wrigglingly evasive as the live eels in a fishmonger's wire basket.

At one point, after I had assured her for the umpteenth time that I wasn't secretly recording her, she announced: "I don't, of course, want what I've just said to be repeated. It's strictly for your ears only. And you mustn't discuss what I say with my daughter."

I was now beginning to realise that I could never have given the lecture if I had known of these revelations beforehand. I could, I suppose, have shown the films and the slides, but, if under prohibition, I couldn't have proceeded with any useful speculation. I pointed this out to Kathleen (in some exasperation) and she instantly turned even more titteringly coy.

"Oh, but David, I think you're a very good lecturer! I listened to the lecture again this morning." (She was referring to the cassette I had sent her, before the lecture, of the far from perfect "dry run" I had extemporised.) "I can only tell you that you alone have set my mind at rest. I'm honestly grateful. I think your theory is absolutely correct. Such a load off my mind! It's even helped me to remember what things were really like after we got the news from the hospital. The only person who wasn't crying was me and I've felt so guilty about that."

She stopped the tittering and her voice cracked during that last sentence. I hastily said: "Thank you, Kathleen. I quite understand."

"Let's put it this way," she said, smiling again. "You can say what ever you like when I'm dead and gone. But not until then, David. That's fair, isn't it?"

"Absolutely fair," I said, "if that's how you want it."

"And, of course," she quickly said, "after my daughter has joined me. That's fair, too, isn't it?"

"Of course," I said, and, more than a shade satirically, I added: "What about your son-in-law if he's the last to pop off?"

All the son-in-law merited, it would seem, was a shrug and a renewed titter. I had further questions to ask about the family

113

reaction to the hospital news, but I decided not to ask them. As it was, I couldn't really believe some of the things she had told me earlier in our acquaintance. Lydia, the maid, had brought her the famous hospital telegram on a silver salver (for instance). It could have been true. But Lydia was what was called a maid-of-all-work. Kathleen's tendency to what she called "romancing" even extended, I suspected, to the delivery of the telegram. Yes, maids did do that sort of thing. But mostly in the movies and on the stage. Fred, incidentally, didn't carry this part of the anecdote in his biography. (It would have been far more important to include, which he didn't, that Lydia often did the shopping for Tressell after the move to London Road, or rather, the shopping for Mrs Beney who did his cooking. That misunderstood choice of London Road had been, in fact, for the convenience of being reasonably near to his sister and his niece Alice.)

And I must also reveal that I never believed Kathleen's story of her aunt being devoted to the constant downing of champagne. It could, again, be true. But was it likely? I think it was more a spiteful reference to imputed extravagance.

I had been so stupid in my youth that I had no wish to force Kathleen into confessing to silly similar follies and even acts of spite. As our friend Mr Pastry once remarked (during the BBC filming when he was giving moral comfort to a young member of his staff): "We all do things in our youth which we wish we hadn't."

Which also applies to Tressell himself. And with the way he thought it best to bring up his only child. We should not forget, I suggest, that he was still a relatively young father when he died – younger than I during this interview (or "encounter") with his daughter. She still had a lingering anger for what, in modern eyes, were bad parental mistakes. In particular, as Fred's biography rightly says, Tressell "told her little" about her supposedly dead mother.

I had never discussed Kathleen's mother with Fred, nor was I destined to after this visit to Bristol. Although he was puzzled by Tressell's reticence, Fred seemed content to refrain from speculation. But I, after uncovering that Kathleen bore the name Elizabeth, a fact that Fred didn't seem to know (although discovering it to have been the mother's real name) was now in a quandary. First, Kathleen was so sensitive on the subject that I thought it tactful not to pursue the whereabouts of her mother's grave. By "sensitive," I mean that Kathleen's eyes could still fill with tears at the thought of the mother she had found herself missing so much.

Secondly, how could I ask her why she had not kept the name? Indeed, the way she signed her name often varied, but never in all the variations did she include the name Elizabeth. I still have the copy of the RTP, which she autographed during her first visit to my flat in December 1968.

She signed herself: *Kathleen Noonan Lynne*, and added "daughter of Robert Tressall" in brackets. The spelling "Tressall" was a little strange, too, considering that she was so familiar with the famous title-page designed by Tressell. It was no spelling mistake. Joan, her daughter, signed herself: *Joan Johnson* and added "grand-daughter of Robert Tressall" in brackets. (The surname "Lynne" was Kathleen's stage-name. Her "real" married-name surname was Meiklejon.) Even Fred, when confronted by these variations – including Kathleen's use of the name "Miss Croker" in her youth – couldn't resist making the slightly caustic remark (in print): "another example of the family trait of cloaking the identity."

What Fred doesn't develop is that Tressell had never even told Kathleen her mother's real name. She had been told it was Madeline (Fred's spelling). But these were as nothing to other inconsistencies.

In revealing some of these inconsistencies, I am not seeking to belittle Kathleen's hardships in Canada. In some ways, even before she deserted her husband, her life was harder than her father's legendary life. Being "on the road" (and with a mind-reading act!) was not only fraught with obvious hazards but actual danger.

115

Nor am I belittling, I hope, the authenticity of Tressell's compassion for what Kathleen called "the underdog." Here is an anecdote, which she failed to tell Fred: her father would sometimes not only give money away which he was carefully saving but even his clothes. He once gave away, in the street, an almost new overcoat. But the fact remains that he was undoubtedly and often so reticent that quarrels with those he loved (and who loved him) were unavoidable. Kathleen herself would, in a rage, burn photographs of him and then, the next day, try to retrieve fragments from the cold ashes in the grate.

Is it any wonder that she began to resort to what she called "romancing?" Is it any wonder that she found it hard to assert her own individuality?

IV

I now come to the last section of this chapter which, even in contemplating it, I find difficult to recount in detail. I can only recall most of our remaining conversation as a series of disconnected bits. A skilled dramatist, I daresay, could weave the bits together, but, even if I were a skilled dramatist, I would think it better to be truthfully vague rather than artificially verbatim at this very delicate point.

Right from 1967 when we first met, Kathleen had been titteringly eager, from time to time, to emphasise how frightened she had been of the male sex. And to Fred, in helping him to complete the biography, she gave equally emphatic examples of how, as a child and growing teenager, she had been absolutely terrified. To me – and not just to my doubting wife – this was inconsistent with her account of her social engagements as a growing girl. She not only spoke of "going to parties" (and annoying her father over the cost of dancing shoes) but travelling in a dog-cart, with other girls, to play tennis in the gardens of big estates. (Her father had her well educated beyond the normal school-leaving age, itself hardly characteristic of a poverty-struck decorator.)

Fred was reluctant to pursue details of her social excursions not only because they "didn't fit" but because, it would seem, one of them was on the big-house estate where his own father had been employed as a gardener-factotum. (Fred had himself lived as a child on this estate.) But, to judge from his portrait of his father in Fred's two semi-autobiographical novels, Fred should have appreciated that his father would have been delighted to know he once drove the daughter of Robert Tressell in a rural dog-cart. Unfortunately, to Fred, this was demeaning. He therefore mentions the occasion only in passing and missed the opportunity to understand Kathleen in greater depth – to say nothing of understanding himself and the origins of his chip on the shoulder.

I am not suggesting that Kathleen was not terrified of the male sex. I am simply saying that Fred should have at least tried to explore the reason for the terror. Surely a biographer's duty?

I cannot remember at what exact point it was that Kathleen again began chattering about her childhood fear of men. I can only tell you that I, even to my own surprise, interrupted her to say: "Are you sure it wasn't just other men you were so scared of?"

I think it was to her own surprise as well that she instantly replied: "I think it was really my own dad I was more frightened of."

She just as instantly clapped her hand over her mouth before removing it and tittering: "David, I never thought I would ever say a thing like that. But it's true. My goodness me ..."

"Perhaps you're the one who needs to be psychoanalysed," I daringly said.

"You could well be right," she said, and her eyes were like two faraway dots of dancing merriment.

To me, this was a quite fascinating glimpse of life-long femininity in an old lady. I had never before seen her looking so happy and relaxed.

Not only surprised but puzzled by this reaction, I asked her: "What in particular frightened you about your father?"

"Simply," she tittered, "that he would find out why Aunt Addie used to spank me. I did mention to Fred that she spanked me. It was with a ping-pong bat but I didn't tell him that and how stingy it was. She was good at ping-pong. Could have been a champion. I was very, very glad when she left us."

Something told me not to treat this confidence in her own merry and almost comic manner. But that it was vital not to be solemn or pompous. Casually, therefore, I asked: "What did she spank you for?"

She replied instantly: "Fibbing."

After a moment, Kathleen added: "She was very strict about fibs. She used to spank her own boy for much longer if she caught him out. He used to cry. I never cried, but he did." (This was a reference to Aunt Adelaide Rolleston's son Arthur who was to be killed in World War One. You can find his name on the War Memorial in Alexandra Park where this oddly lop-sided little family used to stroll.)

"I don't know why," Kathleen further said, "but I seem to cry more easily now that I'm old. I can even cry about Arthur, but I didn't care for him all that much when he was living with us with that particular auntie. Terrible to think he was killed. I was never very much in touch with either of them after they cleared off. Hardly at all."

I think it was at this point that Kathleen revealed that it was her father's smoking, which led to the break (which I've mentioned earlier). I can't be sure. I can't be sure, either, when she said (without any prompting): "I really loved it when we moved to two-four-one." (This was her way of referring to 241 London Road, Tressell's last local address.) "I really did feel I'd got him to myself at last. So many hangers-on used to come to the Milward Road flat. A lot of people, including the BBC, still think Milward Road was the most important place in our lives. It wasn't. We were only there, Dad often said, to give me time to grow up. It had always been Dad's plan not to settle in Hastings. As Alice even told Fred, Dad was a true rolling stone. But, of course, Fred hasn't been able to accept what that means. With Dad, everything he did was planned well in advance. He wasn't a careless rolling-stone."

It is a fact, incidentally, that 241 London Road only received its commemorative plaque very belatedly. It was unveiled by Michal Foster MP, who, it has to be said, knew little about its significance. (I didn't attend the ceremony.) Today, in viewing the house in a busy main-road thoroughfare, enthusiasts perhaps don't realise that 241 was in a far quieter and cleaner road before two world-wars. But I'm not blaming Mr Foster for not knowing the significance. Like everyone else, including me, he had been led to believe, from the legend, that Tressell had been reduced to almost total poverty in 241. Perhaps in a rat-infested cellar?

I can't remember at what point Kathleen told me, during our "encounter," that her father only did a certain amount of work "to keep his hand in" as well as to oblige former employers who still valued his skills. It could never have been true, as I'm afraid Fred tries to perpetuate, that Tressell was treated with contempt by his employers. Even in my own lifetime, a dearth of well-educated, well-spoken people always ensured that "educated" people were viewed (and treated) with a certain amount of deference. As an educated man who had experienced responsibility in South Africa, as well as authority, Tressell would never have been routinely treated in the way Owen, the fictitious character, was treated. He would, at Milward Road, often come home and jokingly say that he had "nearly got the sack" for asserting his former authority. Kathleen told me that he would usually "laugh his head off" in speaking of his interventions.

She also told me that she herself, when still a child, seems to have had the privilege of meeting a model for the immortal Misery. A lanky man was on his bicycle when he got off it in Kenilworth Road and addressed Tressell perfectly politely (and

119

after raising his hat to the very young Kathleen and saying, "Good afternoon, miss.") He wanted to ask, it seems, if Mr Noonan would be interested in an "extra-special" – this being the name for a commission requiring "my valuable talents" as Tressell would ironically call them. Afterwards, Kathleen asked who the man was and Tressell had apparently said: "Oh, just one of my masters," but he did explain that the man on the bicycle was a foreman, and he explained that he himself had been a foreman. I don't know if Kathleen told Fred this anecdote, but, knowing of Fred's integrity, I doubt it. (Fred would have mentioned it.) Putting it mildly, Kathleen had been extremely ambivalent with Fred. Why? Why? WHY?

Thumbing through Fred's book, during this anecdote, I spotted the section where he mentions Tressell's new business-letterheads for 241 London Road.

I asked: "Why did your father add the word 'blueprinting' to his title as a signwriter and decorator? Surely he didn't make blue-prints?"

"That," said Kathleen, " is just another example of Fred's stupidity. I never told Fred any such thing. I simply told him that the letterhead was printed in blue – in blue ink! Blue was Dad's favourite colour. He used to say it was the colour of hope, being the same as a beautiful blue sky. Now, of course, all the world thinks, as you stupidly do, that Dad made blue-prints. And, of course," she said, jumping up restlessly, "Fred and that man Gower wants everyone to believe the rest of our pathetic income was from inscribing-up coffin-plates! I ask you – blue-prints and coffin-plates! How can people come to believe such rubbish?"

"Perhaps," I mildly suggested, "because you didn't altogether make things clear …"

"Oh, I often made things very clear," she said, sitting down again with a thump. "But did it make any difference? Dad never needed or wanted to do much more work in Hastings. All he wanted to do was to finish writing his book in peace and quiet. But Fred wouldn't accept that. He preferred to believe Mr Gower because Mr Gower said otherwise. I told Fred. I said the book had been written at two-four-one. But Fred still hasn't really accepted that."

Kathleen was getting so indignant that I thought it best to get off the subject of Mr William Gower. I couldn't entirely reject his testimony, but I would still agree that it contained many discrepancies. He had even claimed, as Fred faithfully reports, to have been the model for Bert White, the poor little apprentice-boy; but as Kathleen could prove, he was too old to have been the inspiration for that role; and, inapplicably, he had been an apprentice-electrician at the Gaiety Theatre (just off Wellington Square).

As soothingly as I could, I falsely said: "Kathleen, I totally agree with you about Gower."

She instantly relaxed again and got her breath-control back, but she was still a bit indignant.

I did ask, however: "But there's no denying, I suppose, that your father did inscribe coffin-plates?"

"They and other things, yes. As a favour. Not as a major source of income! He was too busy working on the book. He wanted to get it into good shape before he went to Liverpool. He'd PLANNED to do it – had savings."

May I be frivolous for a moment?

I have never been an angler of any sort and I don't understand the pastime. I can only say that I have always admired the sturdy individuality we see in anglers who can sit (and even stand) for so long in Quaker-like silence.

Until they get a bite.

As with them, as with Kathleen. I quite thought I was like an angler in being about to reel in a nice big fish. This was absolutely unknown information. Could it be that Angela had been right? That Kathleen was about to reveal that her mother had blessedly not died and had been living in Liverpool? That Tressell had gone there in the hope of reconciliation?

I sat forward (we were facing one another) and said to Kathleen: "Do you actually know the real reason why your father went to Liverpool?"

"Of course I do," she said.

Her face had gone quietly blank but I was prepared to risk anything for a full answer. As gently as possible, I said, "Then why did he go there?"

Her face tightened a little as she replied; "To get away from me, of course. Me."

To say I was taken aback by this answer would be inaccurate. I was, I must confess, disappointed for a second or two. It was like being the angler who reels in just an old boot or something.

I have already stated that I had decided not to ask Kathleen anything about her mother (and, as far as I know, Fred never asked her about the location of any grave.) But I have to say, disappointed as I first was by the lack of information about her mother, I was now to be astounded nevertheless.

Again, she prefaced it all with: "Are you sure you're not recording this?"

Again I reassured her and she said: "I know it's true because I heard Dad talking to my aunt. I heard him say he couldn't stand my bad behaviour any longer. We'd had a simply terrible row before I heard him say that. David, I'm the one who made him go off to Liverpool before he needed to. I'm the one who caused him to worry and to go off and catch some bug or other which killed him."

"Kathleen," I fatuously said, "it does take two to make a quarrel. You're surely not still taking the blame for his death after all these years?"

"No matter how long ago it was," she firmly said, "I am still guilty. Basically to blame. Louie" (the aunt's companion) "had second-sight. She said no good would come of going away to

Liverpool. She was right, wasn't she? She actually warned him not to go. I heard her say. I was listening."

Knowing how futile it is to argue with even the most congenial of superstitious people, I thought the best thing to do was simply to ask: "But why did he need to go to Liverpool at all?"

"Oh, what does that matter? Just some sort of business. He never ever said what it was. Except, probably, to Alice rather than me. We never really liked each other. She was, I suppose, more intelligent, more perceptive even though she was blind. Even she thought of herself as a Croker."

She rambled on like this while I was looking through Fred's book.

"Kathleen," I said, very politely, "the story is that your father went to Liverpool to find work – enough work to enable him to pay for your fare, and his, to go to Canada."

"Anyone with brains who bothers to think," she said, and equally politely, "could see that's utter rubbish. He already had money for the fare. All that stuff Fred wrote was tangled up by nice people who didn't really know anything about us. Guesswork and gossip. Fairy stories. Fred just lapped them up. That's why we wanted you to take over and tone him down a bit. But you, David, refused."

"Frankly, Kathleen," I said, "might I just ask how far you would have wanted me to go? Would you have wanted me to include things of the kind you're now talking about? Fibbing and so on?"

She didn't reply to this question, except to say: "David, you're beginning to sound like Miss Pope. She cross-examined me as well, for ages."

"With some justification, it seems to me," I couldn't resist saying, and with more of a hint of reproof.

For those who don't know: Miss Jessie Pope was the first person to urge Grant Richards to publish the RTP. She undertook the editing. Henceforth, Fred was always to refer to her as having "butchered" the manuscript, but I think we can forgive him for that. Fred was always going to be Fred. I had myself seen and handled the letters on the subject of publication. It was obvious from them that Miss Pope was both enthusiastic and conscientious … and in ensuring, as best she could, that Tressell (whom they all pronounced 'Tressawl') had genuinely been a working-class man. She obviously had her doubts.

Having found the pages I was looking for (already covered in marginal protestations from the year 1973), I began to give Kathleen a bit of a grilling.

"You actually say here, and Fred quotes you, that your father went to Liverpool to earn the money for your sea-fares. Are you now saying Fred has falsely misquoted you?"

She wriggled, I must say, rather uncomfortably. But not for long. She soon coolly said: "It's true I told Fred that. I went along with a lot of things like that."

"Why? Was it because you were getting paid?"

I thought she would be angry at this gibe, but, instead, she simply smiled. "To some extent, that's probably true. Being offered money and taking it does tend to be embarrassing. It puts one under an obligation. That's why I didn't really want to be found. Until I got to know your wife and you of course a bit better, I just didn't want to be too bothered about what really happened. I agreed with what I agreed with to stop myself from going even more mental."

"Mental? You mean mad?"

"That's what they said about me after I got the telegram from the hospital. Said I'd go mental if too much fuss was made about things. Mad, yes. That is the proper word. My goodness me …"

Her voice faltered a little and I unpleasantly said: "What's the matter now?"

"I've only just really realised how beastly I was to my poor auntie. She had given birth to six children, don't you forget Mr Haines! To take me on, although I was what's now called a teenager, must have been a real burden. I even accused her of stealing Dad's post-office money. My goodness me … I'm remembering all sorts of little things, snatches as it were of things said. David, the reason why it was decided not to anything about the burial was because they thought it would push me right over. Over the edge. An awful scene. Dad, of course, was partly to blame for it all. They were very angry with him for giving my name – me, legally still a child – as the person to be notified. I remember her crying out what could he have been thinking of? Did he want to drive her mental?"

Kathleen was showing no sign of any great distress after this quite long speech. She even ended it with a little laugh and another "my goodness me …"

It had indeed been a puzzle (to those of us puzzled by Tressell's many quirks of character) that he would leave Kathleen in a position to deal with his possible death. ("I wash my hands of him," his sister, Kathleen's auntie, had apparently finally burst out.) It seemed almost as if it had been a fatalistic thing to do. Fred, of course, was clearly of that opinion. He claimed that Gower had received letters from Tressell, from hospital, saying that he "would be glad when the end came."

Kathleen was very annoyed about this insistence of Fred upon this particular testimony. ("Why is it that Gower never produced any such letters? They wouldn't have been letters he would have thrown away, would they? Or deliberately burnt - as I did with some of Dad's letters!")

I can only guess, but I think that Kathleen, in her confusion, "went along with things" more as a way of crushing down the guilt she had felt in causing her father to go to Liverpool before he had planned. In no way did I attempt to explore this theory in the latter half of that momentous afternoon. I thought it simply best to let her ramble on and come to her own conclusions. I had never before in all my life had this sort of a conversation.

Letters do, of course, get lost accidentally and, perhaps, one day the letters Gower claimed to have received might well turn up. Meanwhile, with hind-sight now that we know Tressell divorced the wife and mother Kathleen couldn't remember, I merely suggest the following sidelight on the "fatalistic" view held by Fred.

Fred did, in fact, misquote Kathleen in one particular part of his book (page 161 of the hardback edition.) He says that Kathleen made this "curious remark" about her father: "When he gave up after finishing *The Ragged Trousered Philanthropists* he died."

It was Jessie Pope who made the remark, not Kathleen, but it implied that Kathleen knew of her father's "fatalistic despair." She did not, and, as I mentioned earlier, she was in a world of romantic day-dreams while Tressell was in hospital. (Fred, I'm sure, didn't deliberately misquote. It was simply a biased aberration.) But there can be no doubting the fact that Jessie Pope's personal preface to the abridgement she made (the Pope Abridgement as I have called it) was the start of the "fatalistic" aspect of the ensuing legend.

Could Tressell really and truly have thought he would die in going off to Liverpool?

Not, I suggest, if we take into account what we now know about his matrimonial misfortune.

Even in my own lifetime, it was not considered wise or even moral to inform one's children of sexual infidelity. I can still remember, myself, how few divorced people I knew and how, if someone were known to be divorced, they were always spoken of in a lowered voice. As for any actual divorce, as I knew from my own marriage, even a quiet discussion of it by married couples with children in the offing was rigidly taboo. The phrase "not in front of the children" was a living imperative and not a joke even as late as 1975. Furthermore, if you were married, you did your best to make it work if there were children. Today, these attitudes seem almost insane to modern couples, but that's how we were.

Let us imagine, therefore, how much harder it was – in Tressell's time – for a divorced father to speak to an impossibly shy daughter (who had no sex education) about his divorce and the reason for it. It was actually thought morally preferable, in those days as well as in mine, to tell a lie to a child rather than to speak of something so dreadful as divorce. The lie would always be excused on the ground that it was "only a temporary expedient" and that all would be "put right" once the child was mature enough to understand grown up misconduct.

Tressell was himself a child of his time and I suggest he fully intended to tell Kathleen the truth when he considered it was right to do so. That being so, if it were so, then he would not have "gone off to die in Liverpool" and left his daughter in ignorance. He must have fully expected (and indeed planned) to enlighten her in due course.

But, again, I am not altogether holding Fred responsible for the belief that Tressell knew he would die and even wanted to die. I still have a copy of the only known page from a letter Tressell wrote to Kathleen from hospital.

Kathleen regretted having shown Fred this page, and, frankly, had she consulted me about so apparently desperate a communication I would have advised her to refrain. The whole letter had contained moral admonitions, which were on pages she burnt. She only possessed the last page which, because of its jocular tenderness, she had preserved. But she never told Fred that. She simply allowed him to see that last page out of context. It gave every impression of a man who could be classed as a suicidal risk. You will need to read *One of the Damned* if you want to read the whole of that last page for yourself. Fred quotes this valuable page in its entirety but I will quote only the very last sentence (which is typical of the whole style).

> "… I cannot write down here all that
> I feel and want to say to you but if it were
> true that circumstances compelled us to
> live apart from each other permanently –
> then I would much prefer not to live at all."

We have three choices if we read the whole page (and even if we only read the above sentence.)

We can assume, as Fred instantly and avidly did, that everything William Gower had said about Tressell was true. Gower, of course, had not lived long enough to see this "incriminating" page – incriminating, I mean, in that it "proved" to Fred that Kathleen was a cold-hearted bitch ignoring her father's despair.

Or we can assume, as Angela initially did, that Tressell was putting heavy emotional pressure upon his daughter. ("It's pretty much an incest-thing," she had declared, after reading it. "This is no ordinary letter from a father to his daughter. It's more like a love-letter to a sweetheart.")

Or we can assume this page to be an example of all the jocular but sincere expressions of tenderness in all of his letters from the hospital.

Towards the end of my "encounter" with Kathleen on that day in Bristol, I questioned her about her other letters from Tressell as keenly as another Miss Pope. I also questioned her about her own. His had all been in the same vein, and his had included ironic Latin tags as well the French expressions father-and-daughter had often shared, such as the one after kissing her goodnight – even after their fiercest of quarrels (*je vous aime toujours*). My own French is not good, but I particularly liked the one *Les absents sont toujour tort* ("the absent are always in the wrong").

But there is an important matter here which Fred missed. Kathleen never told Fred that her own teenager-letters had been fewer and less prompt. Also, she had carelessly allowed Fred to assume this only surviving page to be from the last letter Tressell ever wrote. That was not the case. It simply happened to be a page from the only letter Kathleen happened to keep. She did mention other letters she had preserved, but said they had all been in a trunk which was lost at Winnipeg when changing trains. (This she had told Fred.)

It is also a significant indication that her father's death was in no way expected when we consider that no one, other than Kathleen, had made any effort to keep his letters. But, as far as that surviving page is concerned, I tried a highly significant experiment.

I asked Keith Sykes, a member of the Stables Theatre Drama-Recording Group, to read out the page in two different tones of voice. In one, he was able to make the page sound full of despair. In the other, he made it sound charmingly amusing but deeply sincere. I never mentioned this experiment to Fred. I knew it would only make him angry. (Fred, although his two novels had been performed by actors, never took any interest, as far as I know, in the Stables Theatre, and none at all in my drama-recording publications.)

What was all this telling me? That Fred was himself an enigma who would never understand another?

I was with Kathleen that day for some five hours … it could have been even more. I cannot recall the time of my departure. I was too overwhelmed, I suppose, by her final surprises.

The first of them relates to what Kathleen herself referred to (and was quoted by Fred) as a publicity-gimmick. This gimmick (an American expression) was that 'Tressawl' had been a builder's labourer. No work is demeaning if it's honest, but this was a gross physical exaggeration. A good part of the gimmick was that Tressawl had been working-class and was, therefore, only able to educate himself sufficiently well to scribble out his masterpiece. (It did need, of course, to be edited. There was no gainsaying that on any count.) However, depressed by the rejections by other less enlightened publishers, Tressawl was forced by destitution and illness to "give up" and die.

Fred, in *One of the Damned*, makes it clear that he held Mr Richards responsible for the false description of Tressell as a builder's labourer.

"David," Kathleen modestly and quietly said to me, during my reference to this part of the gimmick, "I am the one who told Mr Richards that Dad had been a builder's labourer. Believe me,

I laid it on with a trowel. I was so anxious, you see, to get a good price for all the work Dad had done on the book. I wanted to have enough money to get away to Canada and marry Paul." (Paul had already departed for Canada, and as I mentioned previously, Kathleen had fancied herself to be deeply in love.)

And so, after her remarks about that vague but determined state of mind, Kathleen again repeated the words: "I really did lay it on – with a trowel."

The very expression "laid it on with a trowel" is ironic, in that it relates to the building profession in the most vivid way possible.

"Fred," Kathleen went on to say, somewhat dreamily, "never seems to have realised that I was romancing when I spoke to Miss Pope."

I stood up to say, and severely: "You mean you told lies."

For a moment, I thought Lady Bracknell was about to reappear in all her haughty glory, but no. Kathleen broke into the most beautiful smile I had yet seen on her face. It made her look incredibly (and mischievously) younger.

"Well, yes," she said.

And she got up and kissed me on the cheek.

"Bless you," she added, and turned away to tidy things up in an absent-minded manner. As Miss Pope had said (in the Pope-Richards letters,) no one could want to do anything to harm the daughter of the man who had written such a book.

I sat down again, feeling I had been a pompous ass. She picked up the small volume of short stories I had left on the table, then, indifferently, put it down to say: "David, I hope I haven't shocked you."

Feeling even more of a pompous ass, I quoted the moralising Mr Pastry: "We have all done things in our youth which we regret … feel guilty about."

"Oh," she said, in a more lively voice, "I don't feel guilty about anything. What I suppose I mean, if I really think, is that I was guilty of certain things but no longer feel guilty. You, David, have been a very good boy. Thank you."

She sat down again as if having thanked me for having had a dance with her. It was all very odd, but, at the same time, touchingly sweet.

"I think," she said, using the words she had used to Miss Pope (as reported to Mr Richards): "I think I'd better tell you all about it. Just one or two little things. There's a very small matter about the manuscript, for instance."

"If it's that small," I said, thinking of her reaction to the tin-box matter, "let's not bother."

"Oh, but I think we should just clear it up – just between ourselves. I now really want to."

I thought I was merely about to hear something she had already confessed to Miss Pope.

All Kathleen had confessed to Miss Pope, however, (after much "beating about the bush" as Miss Pope expressed it) was that she was the granddaughter of Sir William Croker.

This startling connection with a family title was a trail that Fred had followed with his usual doggedness. (It really does make fascinating reading in *One of the Damned*.) But what Kathleen had not confessed to was the falsity of her story about the famous manuscript. No one, not Miss Pope, not Mr Richards, nor Fred himself in due course, were ever to know of the "small matter" which Kathleen had now decided to "clear up."

May I just outline this "small" matter as it then stood? And, for many people, still does?

Tressell, it would seem, was so angered and distressed by the rejection of his novel that he was about to burn it. Kathleen, as the heroine of this anecdote, was the one who saved it from the flames. After his death in the Liverpool workhouse, Kathleen took the manuscript with her to London – together with her bicycle and all the other remnants of her poverty-stricken childhood.

From there on, Fred is as accurate about the events leading to publication as the facts allowed.

"David," said Kathleen, contentedly smiling, "my father often spoke of wanting to chuck the novel in the dustbin. And even burning it. But he was only joking. It isn't true that I stopped him from burning it. All he burnt up were the masses of re-writes which were left over. I helped him. And to make sure only the throw-outs were got rid of."

"I can understand all that," I said, "because many a writer feels the same way at times. But I can't understand why you've been telling everyone, including me, that you stopped him from burning the manuscript itself."

"Oh, David – are you really this naïve? Can't you see that I needed to feel important? I was very young. Also, of course, I wanted Mr Richards to feel all the more glad to publish a manuscript which so nearly had got destroyed. And, of course, I wanted that to make him all the more glad to pay big money," and she laughed happily before saying: "Is all that a bit clearer now?"

"Is it true, then, that your father never wanted to burn even so much as one page?"

"Now that I come to think of it," she said, and quite merrily, "he did come near to burning just one page. The title-page."

"The title-page? Why?"

"It was, of course, the page he tackled last – not before writing the book, as so many people think. He had some second thoughts about the pen-name and the use of the word 'damned.'"

"What were his doubts about the pen-name?"

"I can't really remember. But I do remember when he was doing the lettering. But it wasn't me who stopped him from burning it. He decided to leave it and think it over later."

I have to admit that I sighed in reflecting that had Tressell destroyed just that one page ... well, we would never have been able to call him Tressell. Nor could we use a word like "Tressellian" in defining his values. Sighed in relief, I mean.)

According to Fred's biography, Kathleen did mention to Fred that her father considered using the name "Croker" as a pen-name, but that's as far as she went in telling Fred about the title-page. I must say this made me struggle to frame my next and most important question about her father.

"Why was it that he didn't take the manuscript with him? To Liverpool?"

"David, my father was very, very methodical. And he expected me to be the same. He left the manuscript with me with some fairly strict orders. I rather resented them, if I'm to be honest. He wanted me to do some copying-out of the alterations he made after the rejection. I got really cross, I tell you that! And I shirked it. Hardly did a thing."

She stood up and brightly said: "Are you going now?"

"I suppose I ought to," was my utterly dazed reply.

Without knowing why, I said (more plaintively than despairingly): "Is it at least true that your father broke up the model airship he made?"

This was a reference to Tressell's interest in airship-and-balloon aeronautics. I still have a typed-out copy of an unpublished article he wrote on the subject (and corrected in his own writing, so the authorship is authentic); but it is, I have to say, a very dull article. No editor would conclude that it showed any potential as a writer. It is Tressell's illustrations alone which show his talent. (In my early career, I had myself written a far duller article for a junior encyclopaedia because I, too, had been fascinated by the same subject.)

"Or was this," I was unkind enough to add, "just another of your dramatic stories?"

Kathleen's mood instantly changed. She looked as if she had just been hit by an agonising thought.

"David, that was all terribly true. He scared all of us. A simply terrible rage. Honestly, it was the first time, I suppose, that I realised he was capable of rage and violence. As all men are, I came to think. Probably it was the start of when I got really frightened of men. My goodness me ..."

133

Kathleen was here revealing something about herself which was new information, but the actual destruction had been explained in Fred's book in 1973. Tressell, apparently, had been disappointed by the rejection of his design "by the War Office." But psychiatrists would surely say that other disappointments contributed? If they would say that, I'm sure they would be right. Surely they would not assume that Tressell had not been so unbalanced as to react so violently solely to one disappointment? (Frankly, I doubt the War Office was ever approached.)

Kathleen's reaction to her memory of this event would, I suggest, have interested any psychiatrist.

She just instantly changed back to her previous mood, quite frivolously. She tittered and said: "I expect that's why I thought other people would swallow what I said about him wanting to burn the manuscript. Tee-hee! I was being very naughty, tee-hee! No wonder Aunt Addie used to spank me!"

It was during this tittering that she again picked up that volume of short stories. She said: "What's this doing here? Where's it come from?"

I explained that Angela had suggested she should read George Gissing's story *A Daughter of the Lodge*.

"Oh, really?" Again she put the book down indifferently. (I doubt if she knew the name of that author.) "You're a good boy, David, but it's time for you to go. I have my reputation to think of, tee-hee!"

We shook hands rather lingeringly. I was becoming not only more dazed but dry-throated. My brain had almost ceased to work, but, just before she opened the door, I said: "By the way, Angela also said something else. She said that all women are at the mercy of their own bodies. She said you would understand what she meant. Do you?"

"Of course I do," said Kathleen, instantly changing mood again and ceasing to titter.

Again, too, she suddenly looked a lot younger than her true

age. She went on: "Do you think I've never known what it's like to lose all control? To want to lose all control? To love another man I shouldn't love? To have so much to lose?"

There was an amazingly feminine dignity about her as she uttered these words, but, again, her mood and tone changed just as instantly. She again began tittering in a quite silly sort of way as she shut the door on me.

"Mad, mad. We're all mad. Moonbeams, moonbeams," were the final words she titteringly uttered that day.

Those last remarks she had made about a possible illicit romance were interesting. She had already hinted at something of the sort to Fred, as you can read in his biography. But I can't say that I was very interested in anything like that. As I staggered away from her door, it was her remarks about the savagery inflicted upon the airship-model which affected me most.

I was no sentimental pacifist on the subject of violence. Despite all the teasing, I was no longer a Quaker although I had never formally resigned. I certainly wasn't like the unresisting Quaker who meekly allowed two teenage thugs to leave him in a wheelchair for the rest of his life. I have only once been attacked in the street by thugs. It left me with feeling no more than disgust in having to call the police. But evidence of violence in people I esteem or in any way love leaves me with a feeling of real horror.

In that feeling, it would seem, I had found in Kathleen something of an everlasting bond.

SEVEN

Yesterday I Arranged Your Flowers

I

I had every intention of returning to Bristol.

My state of mind, as I made for home, can only be described as blindly euphoric. I had lots of other questions to ask this amazing daughter of Robert Tressell.

And, of course, I was breathlessly relieved that I had not ruined everything by clearing off in a huff.

To this day, I cannot remember where I stayed the night. I only know I must have stayed somewhere because my journey home was on a Sunday. I can vividly remember being on a main-line railway-station, but which one I've no idea. I was sitting among family holidaymakers on crowded benches and scribbling so hard I know I missed at least one train. The holidaymakers either side of me, I remember, became so amused by my muttered note-making that I stood up and gave a sort of mini-lecture. (Whether or not this inspired them to read the RTP I can't say, but they were genuinely and happily tolerant.)

On the Tuesday, I received a short and affectionate letter from Kathleen. Although I own this letter, I cannot publish it because of unresolved legal reasons. Legally, I can only report upon what she said but in my own words. These are that she greatly enjoyed my visit and was astonished to find that so much time had passed without our noticing. ("You must have starved.")

She also added that she, the day before writing this letter, had arranged the flowers I had brought her. They had all been tightly budded but were now unbudding.

What better omen could there be for a great future friendship? I still treasure this undated letter. A lot of people have asked me to give them a letter by the daughter of Robert Tressell, as a keepsake. This one they don't get.

I never showed this letter to Angela or spoke of it. She was away when I got home, presumably on some residential conference or other. We often didn't "connect" for that reason and, frankly, my only concern was the completion of my notes and the further questions I planned to ask.

How much, for instance, did Tressell have in his post-office account when he died? How much of it helped to finance Kathleen's emigration? She was extremely cagey about money, but even Fred knew she was no penniless waif when she set off. I don't know if he ever asked her about the post-office money, but, from his biography, it does seem as if he didn't like to enquire. It might have damaged his picture of the poverty-struck decorator, perhaps? Or did Kathleen deliberately exercise reticence? (I'm putting it politely.)

And other questions were now swirling around in what Shakespeare called the heat-oppressed brain.

How was it, I was asking myself, that so many good and honest people had given Fred so much false information? For instance, he was told that Tressell was so poor that he couldn't even buy flowers for the home he made for Kathleen and for her Aunt Addie and her little boy. Another similar tale was that he simply had "nowhere to go" at Christmas and was often therefore invited to partake with a more fortunate working-class family.

"I really can't understand this particular fairy-story," Kathleen once wrote, after the biography was published. Her father had always dressed up in cotton-wool whiskers not only for Christmas at home but for the children at Aunt Jennie's school. Fred's fairy-story simply didn't make sense, but Fred had persisted in believing it.

One other story is just as preposterous but, again, is still believed and repeated. It is that Tressell was so desperate for work that he went to London for six months and trudged the streets looking for a job. Not finding one, he was forced to return to penury in Hastings.

Even before Fred published the biography, I can remember Angela disputing this favourite tale of Fred's.

"For heaven's sake," she said to him, "don't you think his own daughter wouldn't have noticed the disappearance of her own father?"

Fred only very petulantly conceded, but, in spite of that, he "boxed clever" in the biography. He managed to include the false story by leaving the reader to infer that it was true. For me, this more evidence that Fred was truly in agony over the dangers to the "image" he had of Tressell.

The source of the story is, of course, the fact that Fred believed Frank Owen, in the RTP, to be a self-portrait. And, if you look again at the chapter entitled *The Placard*, in both the full text and the Pope Abridgement, you will find that Owen did indeed "go to London looking for work." He then had to return "to his native town" which, of course, was definitely not Tressell's native town.

In my opinion, Fred cannot altogether be blamed for this simplistic misinterpretation. He might never have believed in it if Robert Noonan, the real man, had not chosen to adopt the name "Tressell."

And not only that.

Tressell, as we now call Mr Noonan, had added the sub-title which Mrs Cookson had disputed and which, as I mentioned earlier in this memoir, was a theme in my lecture. Her contention was that his reference to being "one of the damned" was a reference to his bastardy and not his working-class status. Since he had no working-class status comparable to Frank Owen, his compassionate observation was embodied in a fictitious pen-name. In other words, Robert Tressell was himself a fictitious character who himself had lived "twelve months in hell." Robert Noonan, the real man, had been a writer who, if Kathleen is to be believed, had doubts about the pen-name. Had he destroyed that title-page, it seems to me likely that Fred would never have become so dogmatic.

This matter of pen-names, as it happens, was a subject our literary clique discussed on one occasion. Several of the writers present used pen-names (and this included me in my work as a technical writer.) It was agreed by these writers that pen-names helped to make a writer more objective and impartial.

"It's like another hand holding the pen," one lady said, and everyone except Fred nodded sagely.

As far as Fred was concerned, his hero had used a pen-name to avoid being "black-listed" as well as sued for libel. He wouldn't change this opinion even after learning that Grant Richards, the original publisher, would not have published had there been any question of libel.

Apart from these whirling thoughts, I was working on a project as a surprise gift for Kathleen.

The origin of this project was in that very lecture I had given before going to see her in Bristol. A gentleman in the audience had said, at the end: "It's all as interesting as a play …"

Having now reached a level of complete belief in Kathleen's side of the story, and having noted down everything she had revealed, I exclaimed aloud: "That's it! That's what I'll do, I'll put her in a play."

Instantly, I began typing the play straight on to the typewriter. As any writer of any sort can tell you, it's not often that one experiences this degree of white-hot inspiration. The scene, of course, was to be the publisher's office in the West End of London. I felt I had the whole scene (literally) at my fingertips. I had no ambition to be a playwright, but I had written much dialogue for the technical magazines and I had "adapted" quite a few "out of copyright" plays for the drama-recording group. (I had been obliged to do so because, although actors were easy to recruit, writers were not. Writers were very suspicious of tape-recording in the early days. I couldn't even recruit anyone from the literary clique I belonged to.)

I was depicting Kathleen selling the manuscript to the publisher, Mr Grant Richards, and, as you could guess for yourself, I used the title which I've used for Chapter Two of this memoir. ("*Sold for a Mess of Pottage.*") A bit of melodramatic, of course, but, in our drama-recording group, that's what we mostly went for. I had even got two good voices in mind.

And it was, of course, to be in audio only – in other words, what we called drama-in-sound, a bit like a radio-play but with one or two obvious technical differences from that medium. I began this script at about ten o'clock in the morning and I had finished it, after one or two halts and crossings-out, by tea-time. (I even got up at an unspeakable early hour to add extra touches.)

To say I was pleased with it would be a real understatement. It made me feel I had fully integrated myself as a human being. All of it, I hasten to say, was out of my imagination. I had only ever been intently interviewed by one publisher, at the Focal Press in Fitzroy Square (coincidentally near where Tressell had partly lived in his childhood). I simply used that experience to imagine what it had been like for Kathleen in much the same kind of office.

All I had, as research-material, were my notes of the conversation with Kathleen and my copies of the letters which Reginald had given to me.

And, of course, I was only intending the play to be a purely private performance for Kathleen alone. But, in the middle of putting it in a big envelope to send to Kathleen, I had a brilliant idea. I'm not being sarcastic at my own expense. I really did think it a brilliant idea – and not only that, a happy one.

Why not suggest to Kathleen that she and I perform the play ourselves? I could easily take a good-quality machine to Bristol, or, if I needed to, I could hire equipment there. I had no ambitions as an actor, but I did think I could manage to portray the suave Mr Richards.

And Kathleen, I was sure, would delight in playing her younger self … because the human voice, after all, is the one human feature that can stay forever young. And, for drama-in-sound (as for radio plays), there is no learning-by-heart and no dressing up. For all these entertaining reasons, drama-in-sound is truly Invisible Theatre.

Are you by now beginning to get any sense of the fate soon to befall me?

I posted the play the next day and had it back so quickly I thought I'd stupidly sent it to myself.

Kathleen, it then turned out, had used the return-envelope which I had enclosed so that she could send me, at her leisure, friendly amendments.

She sent nothing like that. She simply returned the script with a diagonal pencil-line through every page. On the first page, along the top, she had written: "I don't like this and will phone you."

And phone me she did – or rather, Lady Bracknell did.

II

I don't want to burden any reader with the technicalities of audio drama-recording, but I need to make one point completely clear.

Over the previous ten years, Kathleen had instantly understood the technicalities with little or no need for explanation. Also, in her letters, she sympathised with my frustrations. Had audio drama-recording been around in her earlier days, she would have taken to it like a duck to water. I don't exaggerate. Intuitively, she saw all the social and other applications. ("Oh, to think of what could have been done with the older kids at Aunt Jenny's! A truly invisible theatre!")

She was certain, too, that her father would have been especially interested. Even Fred, in the biography, included the detail that both father and daughter couldn't bear to hear "ugly" speech. ("Dad saw ugly speech as a symptom of social oppression," Kathleen told me, but she wasn't referring to local and genuine dialects and their attractive variety. She meant the unintelligible distortions which are still with us.) This, incidentally, was why she was so offended by that BBC producer's expletive in 1970 and why she was so annoyed by Fred's unwarranted insistence that her father had used "bad" language during his work.

It was, therefore, amazing to me (as well as a bit of a knock) that Kathleen had sent back the script in the way she did.

Although I had by now moved myself and my "office" into the bedroom vacated by my son (who was living elsewhere), I happened to be in the lounge when the phone rang. I had an extension in my "office-bedroom," but Angela, who was stretched out on the settee, looked at her watch and said: "You can answer that. It won't be for me," and so I went over to the sideboard and lifted the receiver.

This was to be the last time I was to speak to the daughter of Robert Tressell.

She sounded as if she were speaking from a desert-island in the South Seas. Merely a bad line, I suppose, but, to me it already sounded as if a tropical storm was blowing between us. I won't tell you everything she said, but here's the gist.

"David, I can't speak for long and I don't want to. I only want to know one thing. Who've you been speaking to?"

"Kathleen," I apprehensively said, "what on earth do you mean?"

"How did you know about the secretary taking down what I

said in her notebook? In shorthand? Nobody knows about that. Not even Joan."

"It's just something I imagined a publisher would get his secretary to do. The whole script is just a novelty – a joke which I thought you and I could record for ourselves. As a private memento."

"And there are other things you couldn't possibly know without being told. Do I have to repeat myself? Who have you been talking to?"

"No one," I said, "except Joan and Reginald and of course yourself. I've read the letters, yes – but that's about all. The whole thing is only intended as a bit of fun. I made it all up."

"Are you claiming to be a clairvoyant? Is that it?"

"Of course not …"

"Then let me tell you this, Mr Quaker Haines. You can write what you please after we're all dead and gone but not before. Unlike snoopy people like Mr Quaker Haines, I do not break my word," and with that she put the phone down.

I was a little bit saddened as well as amazed, but not for long. After all, had I not been through this sort of thing before? Within seconds, frankly, I assumed this latest "huff" would blow over. I even thought I could soon persuade her to change her mind and perform in the drama-recording. As far as I was concerned, she had simply got cold feet over having "confessed" to more than she intended.

As for her suspicion that I must have "spoken to someone else," it was absurd in more than the obvious way. I couldn't classify it as a compliment to my clairvoyance as a writer because all the material about Mr Richards was on record. All I had done was to pick out bits, which I thought would make the script more entertaining. He had said of himself, for instance, that he was "a gambler with a passion for books." I therefore had him saying this to Kathleen. This she had accusingly encircled in pencil. As for another suave remark (also accusingly encircled), this was a mixture of both fact and my imagination.

"Why are we calling ourselves Miss Croker when, in reality, we are Miss Noonan?"

The simple fact was that Kathleen was working as a nursery-governess (wage: five shillings per week or 25 pence in modern coinage) and under the different name Miss Croker. The correspondence proves it. As for having his secretary take down what she was saying (outside the room but in earshot), this was purely and simply to pep up the scene. I actually thought this would amuse her. I had no idea that it had happened, but, impartially, I suggest that any wise publisher, faced with what appeared to be a manuscript in need of provenance, would have taken this type of precaution. (Let us again remind ourselves: he saw a working-class girl but dressed in clothes from Harrods, no less. She was also in the bloom of young womanhood.) Mr Richards, whom she had told me wore a monocle, was not unworldly, but, in my view, he must have allowed himself to be too easily gulled.

Again, the lines where he cautions her against talking to any reporters "from the papers" (and which she also encircled) were simply from his letters to her. I had no idea he had repeated these warnings.

If I have laboured these literary points, it is not only to emphasise their significance but the effect of Kathleen's phone-call upon Angela.

III

"Went off all right, did it?"

These words, spoken from the settee where she was still stretched out, were Angela's first expression of interest in my return from Bristol.

They were very much in contrast to her animated interest in my departure. They were only spoken, moreover, in the interval between turning the page of the Archaeological magazine which absorbed her.

They were words, I would say, of politely casual indifference. Anyone but I, perhaps, would have realised by now that our marriage was doing neither of us a lot of good. But it was a marriage which, although devoid of tender endearments, had always been polite. Without revealing anything about Kathleen that I thought I shouldn't, I therefore politely mentioned only what I thought would interest Angela the most.

"It seems," I said, "that Kathleen was very nearly sent to your old school in Wellington Square."

Angela went on reading, showing not one scrap of interest. (This characteristic was not unusual.)

"She had a friend who went to your school," I politely went on. "The two of them, it seems, were later on enrolled at the pupil-teacher school on The Ridge. Is it possible in any way for you to check this? From old school-registers or something?"

During another interval spent in turning another page, Angela said: "What was the friend's name?"

"Kathleen couldn't remember."

"That's very helpful," meaning it wasn't.

Not another word was spoken until after I had made Angela a cup of tea. Sitting up to drink it, she said, more brightly: "You need to go to Liverpool."

Liverpool is a very long away from Hastings and a city I had never visited. Angela now gave me all the reasons why I should go there. Although I didn't go, I give her reasons because they might be a stimulus for any non-Liverpudlian who, as a Tressell enthusiast, might care to go in my place.

"You need to go there," she urged me, "if you are to get any ideas as to why Tressell went there himself. I can, if you like, write to my opposite number in the Liverpool public library. Go there and study all the newspapers for the period when Tressell was there. Read every column-inch of every paper he himself might have read. You never know where you can pick up a clue. Get the shipping-lists. Study those and study, too, any encyclopaedia –

but not a modern one! Look up Liverpool in an encyclopaedia of 1911 – such as the Everyman Edition. That's the way to pick up a contemporary clue. See things as he saw them. Walk where he walked. Pretend you're actually him."

Detecting my lack of enthusiasm, she broke off and said: "Oh, well – if you won't go, you stand little chance of ever finding out why he really went there. In my opinion, he probably had contacts there – special contacts if, that is, his wife was dead."

My lack of enthusiasm was due to a sudden feeling of futility. Why bother with all this stuff about Tressell's real life? Kathleen, I suspected, was soon to take refuge in her former anecdotes about herself. In this, as it happens, I was right. She continued to write to me as if our "encounter" had never taken place, but, little by little, our letters trailed off. I have about twenty left out of the eighty or so I exchanged over the years. Kathleen died in 1988 and her last letter to me was in 1983 and merrily silly. I just "went along" in same style.

The last time I saw her: aged 90, she had come for the "unveiling" of the Tressell panel at the Museum in 1982. I entered the Museum for the ceremony and came face to face with her. She gave me an angry look. I turned and left without speaking to her or anyone else. I never actually saw the unveiling of the restored panel. It was unveiled, I understand, by Fred, but I never even glimpsed Fred that day.

I'm sorry that I never wrote to tell Kathleen (it's possible she wouldn't have cared all that much), but Angela eventually found the name of the possible friend who attended Angela's school in Wellington Square.

I can't remember the date, but one day I was at work in my office-bedroom when Angela came in and slapped a photo-copy of a school-register page on my desk. She was in one of her silent moods and said nothing before dashing off elsewhere. I have the photo-copy in front of me as I draft this chapter.

It is a typically poor photo-copy of the 1980 period, and is taken from the Pupil-Teacher Register of 1907. It shows that someone called Bertha Constance Morris was enrolled on the very same day as one Kathleen Elizabeth Noonan (both aged fifteen).

The details (all in copperplate writing) are that Bertha Constance Morris, admission-number 123, was born 15/11/1892. Under the heading "schools hitherto attended by the P.T. as a scholar" this girl is given as having attended Wellington College.

The admission-number for one Kathleen Elizabeth Noonan: 125. Date of birth: 17/9/1892 and "school hitherto attended" given as St Andrew's (the school associated with the Tressell Mural church).

Angela never told me how she came by this register-page, but her manner, in slapping it down in front of me, suggests that Fred, if he had consulted Angela more fully, could have had this information before writing even his "thin" Tressell biography of 1952. Several red-herrings less might then have been the result.

For those who are interested: what actually happened to Elizabeth, the wife of Robert? Will we ever know?

Neither Joan nor Reginald stayed in touch with me after the date of the unveiling ceremony. With the wisdom that is said to come after the event, I think they were both baffled by Kathleen but, out of love and loyalty to her, gave me the cold shoulder. I did come face to face with them before I quitted the museum. Both looked sadly awkward and said nothing.

And that was the moment when I realised (as I mentioned earlier) why Kathleen had been so initially unpleasant to me in Bristol.

It's not nice to feel you've been manipulated, but it's all the worse when done by people you like.

IV

Although already in enough of a dazed state after my lecture in 1980 (and before going to Bristol), I wrote on May 21st to the

WEA tutor-organiser (Mr David Alfred). Having held a meeting with one or two other people (tactfully not inviting Fred), I proposed to Mr Alfred that a Robert Tressell Society should be set up. I sub-titled this memo: "a literary, dramatic and political study-course of Robert Tressell, organised by the WEA at the Hastings Adult-Education Centre."

I outlined six sections, all of them practical, and I intended my own voluntary contribution to centre around drama-recording and filming. I was on that day not under any prohibition by Kathleen, and I thought it would be important to research sensible deviations from the legend and properly explain titbits revealed by Joan (such as the bigamy skeleton).

David Alfred enthusiastically took the idea forward under the better title "Robert Tressell Workshop" and got the funding. Unfortunately (from my point of view), I became alienated from this project. This was partly because I was so busy. I was already booked to arrange a three-term drama-recording course for the Bexhill College in September; but the main reason was that the Workshop became totally dominated by Fred's version of the legend. An interesting and useful booklet *The Robert Tressell Papers* was soon published (in 1982), but none of the matters I had raised in the lecture had been developed. I didn't even know the booklet was being compiled until, mysteriously, it came through my letter-box nakedly. Whether or not it was Fred who had pushed it through (possibly at dead of night) I have no idea. He had certainly stiffly autographed it.

I was on good terms with the WEA, but I had no part, either, in the way the WEA organised the subsequent Tressell lectures. I knew nothing, therefore, of the lecture by Mr John Nettleton at the Queen's Hotel on March 28th., 1981. It was entitled *Robert Tressell and the Liverpool Connection*. As I was to learn later, it didn't have as many ideas in it as it could have had, perhaps, if the lecturer had consulted Angela. Again, as I understand it, this lecture (like all the others) were mostly intent upon strengthening the legend. (Fred, I heard, sat in on every lecture.)

I'm blaming no one for wanting to stick with the legend, which had been so craftily enhanced in the office of Mr Grant Richards. But, for me, all this was becoming an increasingly distasteful state of affairs. It meant, I'm sorry to say, annoying more than one or two people who couldn't understand why I declined every invitation to repeat the lecture I had given on May 3rd 1980. Also, I had to decline "loaded" invitations to events which are designed for the benefit of guests keen to shoot Tressell down.

"I will answer no questions on the subject of Robert Tressell," I was obliged to chant until, at long last, people got the message. Unwisely, and probably because Angela had arranged for it, I did address a small audience of Open-University "mature" students in a hotel-basement. It gave me a severe headache in having to skirt around the aspects which Kathleen had barred. (I don't recall the date and have only one undated page of my grudging lecture-notes.) Fortunately, the mature students (if I may say so without offence) were not like keen-as-mustard Socialists. They were not even very interested in Tressell. I was able to get away with saying as little as possible and I left the premises muttering "Never again." (The fee was paltry, almost an insult, but I was glad not to have earned anything greater for the worst-delivered lecture of my career.)

It was during this period of distaste and frustration that I had the joy of finding what I was ultimately looking for in Tressell.

Meanwhile, it was to give me no pleasure to hear that the Tressell Society (or "workshop" as it was named) was beginning to run out of steam. In my opinion, and like the Tressell lecture-series, it was bound to do so for two basic reasons.

(A) It would not venture beyond the legend; and (B) it did not promote Tressellian values in the shape of practical applications.

May I hope the above paragraph won't be misunderstood?

To stick to the legend, no matter how inaccurate it is, can

only damage Tressell's values if the legend confines its supporters too rigidly to past injustice. In strictly literary terms, it doesn't matter one jot if Tressell had been a poor labourer who died in the workhouse. It doesn't even matter if he had been a prince of the realm in disguise. Either way, a modern form of democracy needs the values which Robert Noonan, the real author, set out.

Having no theological theory to offer, I cannot share Reginald's view that class-hatred is a sin. I can only see it (together with other forms of political hate) as a dark cul-de-sac. My object in suggesting a local Tressell Society was to encourage entry to a wider and better-lit avenue – perhaps leading to a National Foundation.

Inspired by the example of Lional Bart's "Oliver!" I also began to draft RTP lyrics for a musical. The Immortal Misery, of course, was to have the starring role. (Irony, you see.) Just a pipe dream … it's the sort of thing you indulge in when you see council-housing estates being turned into deserts of uncaring squalor (even under Labour governments).

I didn't confine myself entirely to theatrical day-dreams. I also set out to goad the authorities into taking action about the increasing squalor on my own estate. I went around photographing the dangerous lack of repair, the rubbish-dumping and the dog-mess which was ruining the character of the otherwise excellent estate. (It was so well-designed that it had initially won an award.)

I submitted my "report" to the Housing Corporation in London, to the Institute of Public Policy Research – as well as to the local Council and the Labour Party and the WEA.

I submitted many practical suggestions, but my main suggestion was that the term "Social Housing" should be abandoned. It is an insipid term.

All housing is "social" whether private or public. I therefore suggested the term "Democratic Housing" because it demonstrates, more strongly, the idea that public housing is a social right.

I was not suggesting that a government should necessarily stop assisting private right-to-buy schemes if they so chose. I meant it was undemocratic to reduce the stock by selling off public housing merely to attract votes. Am I misjudging Mrs Thatcher, the begetter of this policy? Perhaps. But she was thus preventing the "democratising" of these squalid estates. In other words, she was preventing any idea of the tenants running them for themselves. To mix public and private housing (where the housing is compacted into one estate) can only perpetuate social division and continue the squalor.

What happened to my little report?

On the whole, it was received with good-humoured indifference, but I don't regard the exercise as a wasted effort. It at least taught me to be cheerfully cynical. I realised that opinions, whether hare-brained or not, are only ever going to be as important as the person offering them.

"Now you know where you stand," said Angela. "Try doing some proper writing for a change."

Much as I appreciated Angela's wit, I have to reveal that Social Housing is now in far worse a mess than ever before. Today, it would not be possible for me to write of "good-humoured" indifference. Social Housing is now an industry on a Napoleonic scale. There are still some humane and sincere people within it, but, as I know from some of them, they often feel helpless. A top-heavy structure of petty officials (most of them unseen by the tenants) maintain the old spirit of the poor-law guardians. I am left wondering where Tressell would have put them (in one of his famous oblongs) if he were writing of them today.

He would also, I suggest, be dismayed to find that Equalities Legislation (introduced by Labour) is now so dogmatically applied that it exploits and even endangers the vulnerable.

And, although I'm sure he wouldn't expect all Socialists to go around in sackcloth and ashes, how would he feel about Socialists so wealthy they squelch with money as they walk?

Part Two

Pursuing the Values

EIGHT

Just Telling the Tale

I

At a time when I had a one-man business in Hastings (to subsidise myself as a writer), I found myself unable to pay the rent on my workshop.

To alleviate this problem, I went into the nearby Alexandra Park and sought out the Director of Parks and Cemeteries, Mr W. Cassidy. I asked him if he could give me a temporary job. I had learnt to scythe in one of my former youthful jobs in London, having been taught by a countryman scythe-hand. (With him, I had scythed the fire-break lanes in woodlands near Blackheath.) I had actually brought my own scythe with me, to Hastings, and I offered both it and my skill to Mr Cassidy.

He took me on, not as a scythe-hand but as a park-labourer and I can only say I remain grateful to this brisk but kindly man.

Why had I found myself in difficulties? I had been over-trading. It's a common hazard, but I didn't even know what it meant – let alone the remedy for it. Like most "educated" people of my generation, I had not been taught what are now called "business-studies" by educationists. Most schools (even private ones run by the Quakers) tended to think "business" far too mundane a subject for young minds. The only information I ever got was in a few words about my future choice of career in a frowningly short interview with my headmaster. He advised me, as he did most boys, to "to go into the building trade." For Quakers of those days, anything to do with the arts was "not real work." Yet, inconsistently, it was not thought proper to teach business and commerce. This "moral" view was not exclusive to Quakerism. I was to find, in the Army, that many "educated" boys had been to schools where business was disdained. Even the very word "trade" was disdained in their posh schools.

I was also to find (and still do) that Socialism has its share of people (including teachers) who disdain anything that might encourage the pursuit of private enterprise. To deviate from this "moral" position is to be labelled "a member of the Hard Right" (a phrase I've had applied to myself).

I wonder if Robert Noonan, rather than Robert Tressell, would ever have had been described as a member of the Hard Right?

After all, he did have business-notepaper printed – and in blue. Heinous!

II

I was to learn two valuable lessons from my job for Mr Cassidy which, because I hadn't read the RTP before I came to Hastings, I didn't learn from my previous jobs in London.

Before I reveal these two lessons, may I spend a moment in making Tressell's integrity (as I see it) as clear as I can?

The state of society in his time demanded an account of the most uncompromising type. The Immortal Misery is not only a theatrical caricature. For many helpless and often illiterate workers, Misery was a living reality. Tressell had a writer's duty to expose his sadistic behaviour. The existence of "nice" employers, like the existence of "nice" Germans during two world-wars Tressell had never seen, had to be excluded. For many, Misery was no more a lampoon than the foul absurdity of a Gestapo officer.

This said, may I now report upon what I shall call the Cassidy Syndrome?

I use the term not in the medical sense (a bundle of medical symptoms) but as a bundle of social symptoms creating a class-characteristic.

I personally witnessed and overheard Mr Cassidy talking in the work-yard to one of the employees. I can vouch for the fact that Mr Cassidy, although brisk, was perfectly polite. He showed no disrespect for the employee whatsoever. He was merely asking the employee to tell the foreman about some fallen branches on one of the paths. The whole incident couldn't have lasted longer than a few seconds. I witnessed and overheard it all while being the last (except for this other employee whom Mr Cassidy had detained) to enter our elevenses-hut.

This employee had not noticed that I had seen the incident. He came into the hut where we were having our elevenses (called "bait" by park-labourers) and immediately began giving us an incredibly dramatic account of being delayed by Mr Cassidy.

I won't place before you all this chap said, but here's a rough idea: "Guess what the old bugger sizz to me. Grabs me be the arm and says: you get something done about them branches or you'll get yer bloody cards. I wunt going to stand for that, I can tell yer! I tells im e can stick is bloody job up is arse – and guess what. E crumbles up. Right there. Crumbles up."

"Good for you, mate," was the chorus from the other chaps. "Zonly way to andle im."

Today, I suppose, I would be prosecuted for committing a hate-crime, but I was so astounded that I satirically quoted Shakespeare (the lines from Julius Caesar addressed to the mob): "You blocks, you stones, you worse than senseless things."

They were all a bit startled, then began to grin and chortle as I went on: "Have you serfs and wretched peasants no idea of what's truthful and what isn't? I overheard what Cassidy said. He was being perfectly polite."

There had been, previously, a bit of coolness between these chaps and me, but, after my reproach, they became a lot more friendly. I was regarded, I think, as a bit of a comic mascot. The man sitting next to me was actually shedding tears of mirth.

"Listen, squire," he said, wiping his eyes with a filthy old handkerchief, "it's just telling the tale, that's all. Just telling the tale, see? A bit of fun like. Just atween ourselves like."

From then on, during our work as well as during "bait," I began to appreciate the amazing talent of these chaps for telling the tale. They could take the most trivial incident and build it up in a way that induced real suspense. It could be, say, the toad which one of the chaps found in his garden-shed at home. In telling us all the story and without knowing it, he followed all the rules of the drama laid down by Aristotle and even Gustav Freytag. The story had a proper beginning, a proper middle and a proper end. It was all beautifully controlled (technically speaking). It had, in short, a plot (as writers call it). Here's the spoken climax.

"And what d'you think I bloody saw? Sitting on me private chair where e ad no right to be wore the biggest bloody toad I've ever seen. I swear to you, e wore grinning is ed off like a clown in a circus. Would e move? E would not – not till I picks up me fork. As soon as e sees that, e jumps off me chair and out the door to God knows where."

The fact that I can still remember this tale and others like them is a tribute to the art of the story-teller. But I was soon learning how to spot embellishments. In the toad-story, for instance, I'm willing to guarantee that the fork was an inspired embellishment. The toad probably took far more time to make an exit. It was never threatened with the prongs of the fork. But, as journalists often say (perhaps being of plebeian descent), why let the facts stand in the way of a good story?

The narrator of the toad-story didn't just tell the story. He performed it. He mimed the action with the fork like an actor on a stage.

Does this mean that he and all the others were egotistical liars? I would say not. I would say that he had an instinct for stage-craft (that very close relative of story-telling). He was entertaining his audience – and his audience knew it.

But it has to be said that the Cassidy Syndrome, when combined with this natural ability to entertain, does amount to falsification. Yes, to denigrate the boss can be described as a gleeful form of sport; and even a humane boss has to be philosophic about this form of slander; but it remains a surprise to me that Fred never thought his informants might be dramatising their often faint memories of Tressell at work.

It's even possible that Tressell himself sometimes allowed himself to be taken in by a well-spun hard-luck story. Kathleen told me more than once, in person and in letters, that her father "didn't really understand the working-class." He would come home sometimes amused but more often disgusted and even enraged by the working-class. He couldn't understand, Kathleen told me, why working-class people wouldn't automatically accept what he told them. (The character of the Man with the Scar seems to be an embodiment of Tressell's prevailing bewilderment.)

III

Not having moved in the highest social circles with any degree of regularity, I can only speak of the few well-educated and highly privileged people I have met. I met some of them in the Army and some of them at London parties and just two "fraffly posh" weddings. One social feature was always outstanding.

Except where they have a special talent, well-educated people (even those not of the highest social order) seem devoid of any talent to tell a story. They can gossip, yes; but any ability to construct even a simple chronology is beyond them. It is as if "education" has crushed that sort of talent. The men in particular are still constricted (even in this day and age) by old rules such as: "No gentleman talks about his private life" and "Never complain and never explain." They take pride in adhering to those rules and pride in refusing to acknowledge their real feelings.

It is, of course, normal and understandable for many of us not to be interested in the feelings of people who are total strangers and possibly mad. But this cautious aversion is very different from a quite obtuse refusal to take any interest whatsoever in human nature.

This refusal in some people, such as certain politicians of today, seems almost pathological.

But it's Fred Ball I wish to indicate at this part in my own narrative. (Remember, please, that I am descended from Welsh tinkers. Someone was had up in court only the other day for accusing someone else of having this same low-grade ancestry.)

Fred fiercely strove to stay very working-class. I think you can take that on trust (and let me hope I don't get arrested). But here's the strange thing about Fred. He was not all that good at telling a story. Despite the qualities of his biography, he misses many an occasion to paint a picture for us that we can enjoy. He met Mr Grant Richards, for example, but, both in the book and in his replies to me, Fred was unable to make any kind a story out of his important meetings with interesting people.

Could it be that his zeal to educate himself had somehow crushed down this talent? I can remember Fred being asked about this by others in our literary clique. His lack of a good strong plot in his first novel was the criticism. ("I'm not interested in plotting," he proclaimed, and this, perhaps, was partly why he turned down the offer to contribute to the Sergeant Cork series – which demanded "plots").

After re-studying the RTP and my notes about Kathleen, I eventually got a bit of insight into this "crushing down" of an inborn talent.

It isn't that education in itself crushes down the talent for story-telling. Certain people, once they have been educated, seize upon the idea that "being educated" (and even brainy) is superior to feeling and emotion of all kinds. For variously hidden reasons, these people themselves do the crushing down. And, in doing that, they starve their ability to tell a story. Feelings and emotion are vital to story-telling – and acting – at every level.

Fred, I regret to say, was too much this sort of person, despite the fact that he was a chap you couldn't help liking. Oddly enough for a writer, he had the political lack of interest (already mentioned) in human nature. That remark in his preface about "amateur psycho-analysis coming between a man and his work" is more revealing than might appear.

Indeed, it could be said (and I have heard it said) that to regard our feelings as primarily more important than our intellect is "like turning the world upside down. It's too much to accept."

This discovery is, of course, more complicated than I've made it sound. I was unable to clarify it for myself until after I had read John Macmurray's *Reason and Emotion* (first published in 1935). John Macmurray was the Scottish professor of Moral Philosophy who taught one Tony Blair and was said to have influenced him. It was because of that, I have to say, that I first put my trust in Mr Blair. (Today, I find myself wondering if Mr Blair has entirely forgotten his old professor.)

What John Macmurray had helped me to see was very much a Tressellian value. But it was not the "ultimate" Tressellian value I was looking for.

IV

May I now get back to my experiences of working with the park-labourers? I have yet to explain the second of the two lessons which those experiences taught me. It was something I never dared to tell Fred. It wasn't that I was physically afraid of him, I was afraid, if that's the right word, of being unkind. And I certainly had a sad fear of his potential for violence. I had seen it during the mural-rescue. It hadn't been amusing, for me, any more than Tressell's potential for violence had been amusing to Kathleen (in the savage way he smashed up his "baby" – his airship-model).

This second lesson is, perhaps, of more technical interest to writers rather than readers. I will therefore be as brief as I can, but I would still suggest that it has relevance to any study of Tressellian values.

The simple fact is (and it wouldn't have been seen as flattering by Fred) that Fred's presentation of local speech (in his novel *A Breath of Fresh Air*) is far more authentic than Tressell's.

I discovered this by listening carefully to the speech of those mainly local labourers. They spoke in much the same way as they did in Tressell's time, using the same words and phrases. But Tressell, in the RTP, uses a middle-class form of what is called transliteration. It's the same form used by all middle-class writers, including the writer of *Liza of Lambeth*. It is socially significant that Mr Grant Richards and Miss Jessie Pope didn't spot this obvious characteristic sooner than they did. This seems to suggest the almost watertight nature of class-division in 1913. They hadn't really thought about the way "the lower orders" spoke and wrote (even if the lower orders could write at all).

Fred did not entirely escape this middle-class convention in the way he wrote his semi-autobiographical novel. Even he would use the supercilious apostrophe (to indicate dropped aitches and other letters). But he did get the idiomatic pattern right. Tressell did not. He didn't actually write in what is called Mummerset (the pseudo-dialect used by actors), but his dialogue, although starkly effective, was wholly middle-class in concept. It is the way the middle-class expect working-class speech to be reproduced. Essentially, it is designed for comic effect.

As I've already mentioned, this is a technical problem for any writer. Without resorting to the international phonetic alphabet, a writer has to decide where to draw the line if "uneducated" speech is to be reproduced. If, of course, the writer is writing as a middle-class character, then, logically, he or she is artistically bound to transliterate in the middle-class manner. But I found, on an experimental literacy-course for young local adults, that not one of them, in trying to write, ever used the supercilious apostrophe.

Consider these classical stage-comedy lines:

First pleb: "Arry, where's yer at?"

Second pleb: "Anging on the ook in the all."

Although middle-class publishers won't look very favourably on dialogue reproduced without the supercilious apostrophe, I merely suggest they shouldn't be too pedantic. (I will just add that their compliance with H.W. Fowler's 1928 dictum that dialogue must be in single inverted-commas doesn't just lessen the impact of dialogue. It plays havoc with both the normal and the supercilious apostrophe. American and Canadian publishers, it would appear, never accepted this damaging dictum. As a reader, I can only be thankful. As a writer, I do my best to insist on double inverted-commas for dialogue.)

To sum all this section up, Fred had the better "ear" for local speech, speech distorted through generations of injustice, hardship and cruelty. But I doubt that Tressell ever intended his dialogue to be too comic in effect (although he often thought it so).

By the way, his novel first came out with double inverted-commas for the dialogue, but, prior to 1928, a few publishers were printing dialogue between single inverted-commas only. Perhaps, since they were not obeying Fowler, they were trying to save money by saving ink? ("Thrift, thrift Horatio!")

V

With all this talk about "class," I think I should make my own position clear before I describe my enlightenment (my belated discovery of the ultimate Tressellian value). In local political

163

discussions (which I now avoid), I have found myself accused of being a member of the Hard Left as well as a member of the Hard Right. I don't want you to be as confused as I am by the careless use of these terms.

Long, long ago I told Fred Ball that I believed in a two-class system of society.

"No class and low-class," I told him.

He wouldn't agree. He said: "There will always be a working-class. There has to be. It will always need to protect itself from attack."

I still believe in the division I was unwise enough to mention to Fred. For instance, I shall immediately become Low Class as soon as I become an international jewel-thief. For the moment, I am still No Class.

Is any further explanation necessary? If there is, I decline to moralise. It is for others to decide the modern categories for Tressell's oblong.

As for my enlightenment, it is a shade more complicated, but only in the sense of being a lot more worthwhile as a pursuit. I must, however, issue a friendly warning. You might find it worse than difficult to accept the "ultimate value" (as I found it in the story of Tressell and Kathleen). You might even find yourself in the sensitive position of a limpet fixed to a rock but deprived of its strongly protective shell.

The Ultimate Tressellian Value (which all of us will always be entitled to deny) is only too easy to put into words.

It is simply that a normal, well-balanced democratic nation is like the mind of a normal, well-balanced man or woman.

Or should be …

This idealised analogy will always be far from exact. Many a democratic nation can itself be as mentally unbalanced as any suffering individual. In Britain, for example, we can see this on show in what is called the Mother of Parliaments. This famous phrase was coined in 1865 by John Bright (a Quaker, by the way);

but I often wonder what he would think, today, if he could see the behaviour of this Big Momma on the BBC Parliamentary channel. At various times, she seems to behave in the way my own mother used to behave. Although I loved her dearly, I had to accept that she was quite incredibly dotty. She would spring to her feet at tea-time and start flinging her tea-cakes all round the room. (You had to learn how to duck at a very early age if you were to avoid being hit in the eye.) Although certain members of Parliament don't fling actual cakes, they often fling verbal cakes around in the same wild way.

The Mother of Parliaments has its own species of therapist in the shape of the parental Speaker, but what about the rest of us outside those walls?

Who can be the best possible therapist for the mass of we the "ordinary people" of Britain.

The most appropriate for a democracy is often said to be a free press – or the Media as it is nowadays termed (often pronounced "Meeja"). But the Meeja can too often seem as dotty as the politicians. What else can we conclude from its own bouts of frenzy?

What, then, of the priesthood? Well, not if it is like the two priests who told Mrs Cookson (after she awoke in hospital) that her exhausting miscarriage was God punishing her for her sins.

What, then, of the psychiatrists? Surely they must be ideally suitable? After all, these are the experts who invented the very term "psycho-therapy."

But they, too, can be as sternly dogmatic as any fanatical priests. In my own early efforts to uncover how best to handle Fred Ball, I had only to read of the quarrel between Freud and Jung, to say nothing of the way they treated dissidents, to realise that our psychiatrists themselves are only too human.

VI

I have emphasised the phrase "only too human" not in sadness but with much gladness of heart.

My discovery that even our psychiatrists can quarrel among themselves was, for me, a confirmation of another precious Tressellian value.

Individuality. A democratic right. Inevitably, it leads to splits. It was why Robert Noonan himself, in Kathleen's eyes, was so "difficult" to live with. And it was also Kathleen's individuality which, for him, made her just as "difficult" in being his daughter.

Also, it was Fred's individuality which would have made him as unwelcome in the former Soviet Union as Robert Noonan. Although Fred himself had once been a member of the Communist Party which held the RTP in high favour, I think we can be sure that neither Fred Ball nor Robert Noonan would have survived in Stalin's Russia. Even today, in undemocratic countries like China and North Korea, individualists like Mr Ball and Mr Noonan would be either executed or imprisoned. The only people allowed to exercise individuality in such countries are the dictators (aka tyrants).

The best therapist for a sick society, therefore, is always going to be Democracy – i.e. the right of the individual voters to chuck out their rulers.

But what of the individuals in that sick society who might themselves be so "difficult" or so unhappy as to need personal therapy?

Where can they safely go?

In an undemocratic country, we can only conclude it to be unsafe to go to a state psychiatrist. The suffering individual would presumably be made to conform to the strict politics of the state – probably through drug-therapy or even brain-surgery. But, in a democratic country, sufferers will at least be in good enough hands even among quarrelling psychiatrists.

All sufferers should, of course, have enough common-sense to find out what "school" their prospective psychiatrist supports. The popular myth, encouraged by Hollywood movies, is that all shrinks are all the same in being wise and kind. This myth can cause serious damage. ("Six months of expensive humiliation" is how Noel Coward described his own experience of psycho-analysis.) Fortunately, it is safe to say that most shrinks today, whether they be strict Freudians or not, are safe enough to consult if the sufferer's problem is not as profound as that of Mr Coward's. Even an untalented shrink can be helpful.

I'm giving this advice because, this being a personal memoir, I must admit to having experienced a feeling of hopelessness after Kathleen's rejection of my script. It never occurred to me, I must also admit, that my rather strange marriage was another reason for my feelings of hopelessness. To me, our marriage was marriage and that was that. ("Baloney," was almost as much as I could say about Bristol to Angela and I never told her of the script I wrote for Kathleen.)

In my own case, there were of course "contributory factors" behind the feeling of hopelessness, which came over me whenever I thought over my life as a whole. But, because Kathleen had herself spoken of a need for psycho-analysis (for Angela), I eventually began again to explore the shelves of a secondhand-bookshop. Ostensibly, this was because Kathleen's advice couldn't be followed. Angela gaily refused to see a psychiatrist. I was therefore hoping I could find help for her in the shape of a book. Naively, I was hoping I could learn how to help Angela myself.

By the merest chance, and in the nearby town of Bexhill-on-Sea, I came across the book which was to be the only book, written by a psychiatrist, which tended to equate a healthy democracy with a healthy, well-balanced individual citizen.

This value, as I've already suggested, is more of an analogy than an equation. But I didn't see the difference straight away. I very nearly didn't buy the book. The price was fifty pence for a

1947 edition and I thought that a bit steep. I actually put it back on the shelf before turning back and deciding to give it a go – and risking, for those days, a respectable sum.

I had never heard of the author, a woman. She had not even been mentioned in the other books of psychology I had previously bought and slogged my way through (in my attempt to fathom Fred). Also, at that time, I had no idea that one day I would write this memoir. I was only to write it because, one day later in our lives, Angela said to me: "You should write a book about all that Tressell stuff."

"Too personal," I had dismissively replied.

"That's why you should write it," she said, "come what may and no matter what you need to say."

In having got around to complying with Angela's suggestion, I cannot finish telling my own tale about Tressell without including the genius of a psychiatrist who gave logical shape to my search for the ultimate Tressellian value.

NINE

Some Other Daughters of the Lodge

I

There were quite a few "daughters of the lodge" living in Hastings during Kathleen's childhood in the 1900's.

If you have yet to read Gissing's wonderfully ironic story *A Daughter of the Lodge* (first published in 1906 in *The House of Cobwebs and Other Stories*), I won't spoil your forthcoming pleasure by telling you too much. I'll only say that it's about the "new-woman" of the period, a creature much despised as unladylike and unnatural. And not only by the majority of men. Just as there are today, there were women in 1900 who more than merely frowned upon such immodesty.

It has to be admitted, even by the staunchest of Tressellians, that Tressell himself appeared to have taken no great interest in the emancipation of women. Indeed, his fictional treatment of what used to be called the distaff-side is inferior to Gissing's. It is Gissing you need to read if you want deeper studies of women of that era and more detailed squalor.

Did Tressell ever read Gissing? That, I regret to say, I never found out. Gissing died prematurely at the age of 46 in December 1903, but, having those extra six years (Tressell died at 40), Gissing had completed 28 books. I believe that Tressell, had he lived even a few more years, could have come up with Gissing ladies just as horribly brilliant as Pennyloaf Candy and the others. ("Pennyloaf" is how the lower orders pronounced the name Penelope.)

A brave "new woman" in Kathleen's Hastings childhood was Dr Elizabeth Blackwell who lived in Rock House. This is on the far side of the public open space known as the West Hill. Kathleen and her friends had often played on the grass there (as children do today). Kathleen had probably seen her being pushed in her bath-chair along the paths. This famous old doctor died in 1910 after a long struggle to become a medical doctor and having to endure much ridicule and the disparaging title of "doctress" (rather than "doctor"). I mention her because of her faint link with Kathleen in having been medically trained on the far side of the Pond – the Atlantic. I also mention her (of course!) because Dr Blackwell was one of Angela's historic heroines of women's emancipation.

I also mention her because the author of the book I found in the Bexhill shop had almost the same sort of troubles, but in the all-too ancient University of Freiburg (in the Germany of 1906). Her struggle to qualify was just as heroic as Dr Blackwell's, but, in a sense, even more heroic in that she became a pioneering psychiatrist who had to do battle with entrenched male Freudians. She had, as it were, a battle on two fronts – one being against the prejudice against women as doctors and the other being against the male-orientated theories of Dr Sigmund Freud.

II

Uncommonly for a supposedly working-class man, Tressell had kept Kathleen at school well beyond the usual school-leaving age. (Yes, I've said it before.)

It was while Kathleen was thus being educated in Hastings that Karen Clementina Theodora Danielson was striving to become a medical doctor.

She was German but of mixed national parentage; despite this and a sea-captain father, her family's circumstances were comfortable and highly conventional. Yet Karen Danielson was to become not only daringly egalitarian and socialistic but astonishingly (for the period) sexually explorative. In other words, she was to become a German version of a "new woman" but, of course, in the romantic period of German history before two world wars. She was soon to marry a business-student, Oskar Horney, a member of her liberal-minded circle of friends. (It seems that German universities were not as snobbish about "trade" as British universities in those days.)

Although she was eventually to divorce and emigrate to America, she kept to her married name (Karen Horney) and it was under that name that she wrote the book which astounded me.

As it had a lot of other first-time readers!

It is called *Our Inner Conflicts*, a short but powerfully persuasive book (still in print after all these years. It was first published in the USA in 1945).

Her command of the English language, I would say, is as phenomenal as Joseph Conrad's. She does come out with the occasional jaw-cracking array of words, but I think we can forgive that. (One chapter, for example, is entitled *Auxiliary Approaches to Artificial Harmony*; but all her other chapter-titles are lucidly down to earth.)

"Blimey," I was to cry out, as did so many, "she's talking about ME! And this bit – it's about my brother! And she's even got my old headmaster off – to a T! Even old Fred! Even Mr Pastry!"

For me, this book was far more of a revelation than Dr Jung's book *Psychological Types* which I still have on my groaning shelves. But please don't imagine that I entirely reject the work of Freud and Jung (any more than Dr Horney did). It should be a part of our culture to study their works or at least to have "dipped" into them. It's an intellectual treat, for example, to read *Essays in Applied Psycho-Analysis* by Dr Ernest Jones. I particularly cherish his depiction of our human minds as being pin-points of consciousness in universal space. But Dr Horney's apt references to democracy, throughout all her books, strike me as having more of an everyday application. For that reason, I have to say, I find it tragic that Fred Ball was unable to see any practical use for psycho-analysis as an aid to humankind. A great thinker like Dr Horney should have appealed to him, too, because of her additional (and very well-informed) references to Literature. She could, I suggest, be considered to be the ideal psychiatrist for any creative artist in need of help.

III

Does that last sentence in the above section mean that Horneyian psycho-analysis is only of use to dotty people like painters, actors and novelists?

It does not. But I now have to make a statement which, for some people, will be offensive.

Tressell's exposition of Socialism in his one and only novel may well be a bit out of date ("a museum-piece" the dramatist Arnold Wesker called it). But anyone (whether "working-class" or not) can understand and follow Dr Hornet's reasoning if, as readers, they have been able to understand and follow Tressell's equally clear reasoning in the RTP.

It's true, of course, that Dr Horney writes in a "middle-class" way for "middle-class" readers. She uses a middle-class vocabulary. She is also too fond, in my fastidious opinion, of the word "factor" when she is referring to a reason, an element or even just an ingredient. But she is never as obscure as certain otherwise helpful psychiatrists writing for the public. Jargon comes as naturally to them as breathing. Their very vocabulary can belong, as it were, to another planet. What, for example, does Dr Anthony Storr mean by the phrase "loss of proprioceptive information"? Fond as I am of my big old dictionaries, even my 1842 Webster has let me down over the word "proprioceptive".

Putting aside that minor quibble of mine, may I move on to suggest that you spend just 20 minutes of your life in trying out just one chapter of *Our Inner Conflicts* by Karen Horney?

It might take you only ten minutes to read, depending on any prior experience you may have of reading other psychological tracts.

Because I was in the state of hopelessness I've already mentioned, I went straight into the chapter entitled purely and simply *Hopelessness*.

I'm not going to summarise it for you except to say that it was, for me, an incredible revelation – and not least for the fact that Dr Horney uses a quote from Professor John Macmurray in suggesting how we set about resolving our inner conflicts.

In referring as she does to "the central theme of Zen Buddhist writings," she uses this question by Macmurray in support: "What other significance can our existence have than to be ourselves fully and completely?"

But I don't want anyone to jump the gun if, as can be possible, they don't have any prior reading experience of Freud and Jung and all the others. It may suit you better simply to begin at the beginning. I would only add here that you might prefer to go straight into Chapter One but without reading the introduction. This introduction by Dr Horney is, in these later times, a bit irrelevant. She appears to be a little guilty about having defied Freud and is, ever so faintly, on the defensive. Today, her theories have to some extent been accepted by the Freudians in rather the same way as crusty old Tories have accepted bits of Tressellian Socialism. (I'm speaking in fun here, but it really is a fact that Mrs May, the present British Prime Minister, had an election-slogan which, in earlier years, would have had her listed by the CIA as a communist. The CIA did once list an earlier prime minister, Harold Wilson, as a Soviet spy. It is amazing how the absurd conspiracy to bung him in the Tower of London has been glossed over. Modern Tory leaders, perhaps, need to watch their backs.)

IV

Timewise, this anecdote may be out of context but is relevant here.

A simple failure on my part to help someone, although a total stranger, did not cause the later tragedy; but, if I had been more insistent, I might well have helped to avoid it. De Karen Horney, who had herself suffered suicidal depression, is my guide in her chapter on hopelessness. She tells us that many suicides could probably be averted "if more attention is paid to the less dramatic signs of hopelessness." (Suicides in UK in 2017: 6,188 so far.)

This particular occasion, which was at the Stables Theatre in Hastings, was not in any way dramatic; but, for me, this was a sad social omen.

Angela was the chairman of the Professional-Programme Committee and, through her, I was sometimes asked to meet professional actors or celebrities at Hastings Station. I would take them by taxi to a voluntary host-members house or direct to the theatre (if they didn't need accommodating).

This particular celebrity, Lady Isobel Barnett, had been booked to give the second of two talks, the second being in 1975. She drove to the theatre in her own car and all the way from her very distant village. I therefore had no opportunity to scrape acquaintance with her. I only knew her, as did many millions of other besotted males, as the one-time beautiful panellist on a silly TV show called "What's my Line?"

She had a "fraffly" posh but charming voice and had been dropped from the show, presumably for being "shop-worn" at 58 or perhaps for being "too difficult." Her fee for appearing at the local theatre was probably about £100 (You might be surprised to know how many well–known celebrities were glad to earn this sort of money and sometimes less. But she was no silly female. In reality, she was a qualified medical doctor and had been a magistrate of high standing. These enigmatic details were in themselves a warning sign, but, when Angela told me of them, I only said:

"That's a bit strange. Why should someone like that want to come all this way to give a talk? Surely she can't be hard up?"

I never heard either of the two talks. I was only in the theatre at the end of the last one and I was not in the auditorium. I happened to be in the bar at the top of the stairs. I was awaiting an appointment with a member of the fledgling drama-recording group. A faction of back-stage members was dominating the bar and was ignoring me in its customary way. I have many happy memories, I need hardly say, of this marvellous "little" theatre; but this was not one of them. The faction was not only thinly hostile to professional-programme policy, it was more than thinly hostile to the drama-recording group. (Such were the "politics" of local amateur theatricals.)

I didn't immediately recognise the celebrity-speaker when she came up the stairs after her talk. The faction, being from back-stage, must have known who she was, but, to my disgust, its members turned their backs on her after a quick glance and went on yattering. I can't recall whether this was before or after Mrs Cookson's visit, but it was very like the situation I have previously mentioned when she too was ignored. There being no sign of Angela or any other member of her committee, I moved forward with my glass of tonic-water. I was intending to say: "I understand, madam, that you, like me, went to a Quaker boarding-school. Would you welcome a very Quakerly glass of tonic-water? Or are you in the market for something a little more daring?"

I had no chance to utter this frivolity. The lady had gasped out a wounded "huh!" and was hurrying off down the stairs. I should have gone after her to the car-park, but I'm ashamed to say I did not and thought no more of the boorish incident. I heard later that she had put in for petrol-expenses which Angela and her committee thought extravagant. I also later heard, as did everyone, that she had been found guilty in 1980 of stealing a small tin of fish from her village shop. And for that she had killed herself horribly.

I wouldn't have known enough, in 1975, to recommend advice from some of the magnificent chapters in Karen Horney's master-piece *Neurosis and Human Growth*. But I think that chapters with titles like *The Search for Glory* and *The Tyranny of the Should* and with, perhaps, *Self-Hate and Self-Contempt* would have gone straight to the heart of Lady Barnett's gradual but impending tragedy.

The only quibble I have about the book is that its sub-title (*The Struggle Toward Self-Realization*) should perhaps have been the main title (with the title *Neurosis and Human Growth* being the sub-title). But, provided we understand that people like Lady Barnett have become alienated from themselves (having what they sometimes complain of as a "not me" feeling), we will then have grasped Dr Horney's full meaning.

Just to be a little more pedantic, I would say it's not a struggle *toward* self-realisation but a struggle *for* self-realisation.

And it really is a struggle. Lady Barnett, I think Dr Horney would have said, was in despair at the thought of not being whole-heartedly herself.

Mrs Cookson, I venture to suggest, was in the same boat. She had admitted to Arthur Spencer Roberts, the artist, that she had thought of suicide even at the height of her fame. It is a sad fact that I was not able to suggest to her that she, with all her wealth, could easily have popped over to New York and booked in at the Karen Horney Clinic. Perhaps in Lady Barnett's company?

Anyone who ever speaks of having suicidal impulses does need professional help. Even if they say so jokingly.

But sufferers who don't have suicidal thoughts can nevertheless be having an agonising time. This does require us to take the initiative more than we sometimes think we need to (even if our knowledge is elementary).

V

I can almost hear some people asking why I am "making such a fuss" about a long-dead celebrity – especially as I had no personal contact and, even worse, she had nothing to do with Robert Tressell.

The point I am trying to make, as I hope others will have twigged, is that we cannot hold Tressellian values and dream of a healthy democracy if we regard mental illness as a crime.

Or, if not a crime, then something to be kept secret and to be ashamed of – whether in oneself or in a friend or a close relative.

How can we possibly equate a well-balanced and healthy democracy with the mind of a well-balanced and healthy human being if we can't accept that all mental illness must be openly discussed?

And how can we have that equation – or analogy – if we stay frightened of mental illness?

"So," I hear others saying, "you are expecting us all to become spare-time psycho-analysts!"

I'm not suggesting that, but I am suggesting that magistrates should have learnt enough in their training to understand what psychiatrists mean by "inner conflicts." The fact that Lady Barnett was so far gone as to devise a shop-lifter's pocket pointed to her future self-destruction. Her conviction was not just a piece of ignorant cruelty. It was an injustice.

I am not among those people (very prevalent among Quakers in my youth) who are eager to drape a garland of forgiveness around the necks of real evil-doers. But I can understand how many of us fear mental illness, especially if we've been on the receiving-end of it. As a child of about four or five, I had been cosily transferred to my mother's bed, by her, to aid my recovery from illness. My Quaker father, armed with a stick, came in later. He dragged me from the bed. He was so slashingly violent he made my nose bleed. It was only then that he stopped and strode off.

It was to be years before I understood, from Dr Horney's books, his motive. It was simply that he was jealous of the attention I was getting. My two young but older brothers were treated far worse. My oldest brother never fully recovered from the ceremonial thrashings he had to endure. To this day, I can also remember how he was made to wash his sheets in the front part of the garden (to be seen by anyone approaching the house) if he wetted the bed. About six months before he died (prematurely, but as a highly respected North Country Quaker elder) he said to me: "I cannot think of my childhood without a shudder."

My father was to embarrass me excruciatingly when I was at school. He would, thank goodness, only visit occasionally, but, when he did, he would do things like marching (uninvited) into the staff common-room and saying: "Anyone here for a game of chess?" He would also go round the village and bang on the door of anyone unlucky enough to possess our surname. ("I've called to see if we're related.")

You might now, perhaps, understand why I found Fred Ball's behaviour, during the mural-rescue, to be a too much of a reminder. But at least I was able to recognise, eventually, that such egotistical people are dominated by an unresolved infantile conflict.

Would it have done my father any good to have been prosecuted for cruelty to his three boys?

I doubt it. I suspect he would have killed himself. What he needed was help for individuality gone wrong.

But what I know for sure is that there are still people around (and not only among Quakers) who will say it is in "bad taste" to reveal what I've just written. ("Talking about madness in one's family is an act of betrayal. It's like washing one's dirty linen in public. A lot worse than just rocking the boat.")

Yet "madness" in the shape of unresolved conflicts can not only destroy lives and families; it can, in a collective sense, damage and even destroy a nation.

VI

It's a loss to literary history that I didn't get Kathleen to talk even more freely about the "madness" in her own family. As Angela had noted (and before I did), Kathleen had inclinations, like the heroine in *A Daughter of the Lodge*, to be a well-educated "new" woman. Kathleen herself had assured me, despite in her later life "leaning" to the Liberal Party, that she had been a "red-hot" Socialist in her girlhood. She had remained so during the early short time of her ill-fated marriage to her cousin Paul. After contemptuously saying to him "Tell them I'm dead," she had begun to express her individuality in other ways.

I had only a hint of what she meant, in those last words of hers, before she closed the door of her room upon me. But I'm not going to speculate upon that hint. It's for others, backed up by research, to do so if they wish. Having mentioned her father's individuality – and defining it as a democratic value – I am referring only to existing threats to human individuality.

A "threat" to individuality is, I would say, a threat to democracy (if you accept my thesis).

Consider, for example, the subjugation of women. How can any threat to their individuality be tolerated in any nation claiming to be a democracy? Do I need to give details? Surely not? But the Horneyian Analogy (if I may call it that) can never become an equation if one scrap of female subjugation is permitted to exist. I shall mention some details a bit later on, with, however, much reluctance. That's partly because I'm too astonished to find such references labelled "racist." Irrespective of real examples of racial prejudice, the word "racist" is becoming a term of "working-class" abuse – just like the word "bastard." Mere parrot-cries.

I could give many examples, but one should suffice. A disabled friend of mine was called "a racist bitch" by an able-bodied "working-class" woman because my friend was trying to park in a disability-bay at Tesco's. But just as ugly, to my mind, are the dogmatic examples in Labour Party circles where even a word can be named as "racist" when it is not.

I can only hope that I only need to point out that the idea of men and women "being equal" is nothing new. It was at the core of Kathleen's belief in Socialism, for example, that all men and women are equal in the sight of God. It was not just offensive to her that men and women were not as equal in the sight of men. It was irreligious.

For this reason, I am completing this memoir by writing a separate Part Two. It is inspired by Kathleen and her relationship to her father, but, for me, it is a memory that relates more directly to our need to more candid about mental illness.

And how we personally deal with it – whether close to home or not.

VII

How unhappy was "this unhappy man" as Mr John Manwaring Baines described Robert Tressell?

I am referring to the official letter of thanks, to me from Mr Baines, which I have quoted elsewhere in these pages. What I didn't mention was that Mr Baines had consulted Angela before writing it. Mr Baines himself had no interest in Tressell whatsoever (as another earlier reference in these pages tends to prove). It had been Angela (as she let slip years later) who had suggested inserting the word "unhappy" between the two words "this man."

Like lots of people who take their cue from Fred Ball, Angela had used the word "unhappy" in too general a sense. According to Kathleen, there was a lot of laughter in the home as well as the "dreadful" quarrels. Tressell was far from being the sad-faced figure of his legend. He was often "full of fun" and liked to play harmless practical jokes. He was particularly happy when writing.

But Kathleen qualified this information in her typical inconsistent way by saying: "He was basically unhappy and for one special reason. He couldn't believe in God. Do you believe in God, Mr Haines?"

This particular memory of Kathleen is the one I awkwardly couldn't recall in Bristol. It was of the time when she (with Joan and Reginald) first began trying to buttonhole me about Fred's biography. It was on a separate occasion when they called, uninvited, at the flat. I can only say it must have been well before 1973 (the year when the biography was published). I was alone with these three Tressells and felt alone. Kathleen was being hoity-toity. And so was I. Nothing annoys me more than being asked if I believe in God. I think it an impossibly tedious question by someone who is still almost a stranger. When I'm asked it in the street I usually say nothing; but, this being Tressell's daughter, I decided to give out my standard reply for when I'm unavoidably pressed.

"I do not believe in God," I politely said, "but that doesn't mean that I regard universal reality as futile and meaningless. That's all I want to say, thank you."

Kathleen instantly and icily said: "My father was always saying things like that. Was it his book which inspired your belief?"

"His book," I said, still polite, "certainly helped to confirm my thoughts – if I may put it that way."

"You are entitled," she said, even more icily it seemed to me, "to put your atheistic disbelief in any way you like. But how, without prayer, are you able to judge between the right thing to do and the wrong thing to do? just tell me that, Mr Quaker Haines."

Suddenly, I felt miraculously light-hearted and self-confident.

I said: "As a certain writer says in a certain book, the right thing to do is always the kind thing to do. That's all one needs to remember."

This simple statement seemed to floor the daughter of Robert Tressell. She even seemed to gasp slightly.

She said: "Whereabouts in his book does my dad say that?"

"It wasn't your father who wrote those words," I said, grinning my head off. "It was another writer entirely."

181

"And who might that be, might I ask?"

"Somerset Maugham," I challengingly said. "Have you heard of him?"

"Of course I have," she almost spat, as if I had insulted her intellect, "but I've also heard that he's superficial. Cynical. I wouldn't dream of reading his books. He knew nothing about real life, only the lives of the rich. He knew nothing about the underdog. Nothing about the working-class my father tried so hard to help."

Still daringly grinning, I said: "Somerset Maugham did write about the working-class more than you think. He wrote *Liza of Lambeth* for instance. He had trained to be a doctor. It was only his little black bag which protected him on some of his rounds. Your father, I'm certain, would have appreciated even his later work. It did indeed included the middle and upper classes, but the whole point about his work is –"

I wasn't allowed to finish the whole point (which incidentally, is that even the lives of "our betters" – the title of a Somerset Maugham play – are also real life). The daughter of Robert Tressell gave me what novelists call a baleful look. She was out of her chair in a bound. She shot out of the lounge with her son-in-law in hasty attendance. Before following in their wake along the short hall-corridor, Joan lingered long enough to whisper to me: "Don't worry, David. Mum's often a pain in the bum even to us."

As I have said, I cannot remember the exact time or date of this conversation. These details have floated away into the eternity of all half-lost memories.

I have put Kathleen's view first in this Part Two because she believed her dad's unhappiness to be due, primarily, to alienation from God. She was steadfast in that belief and I am not going to dispute it.

I am putting Angela second in this Part Two because she is relevant to it for several reasons, one of them being that we should try to do the "right thing" for someone close whose reasoning is suddenly more than just strange. But I won't blame any reader for not seeing, initially, how a failing provincial marriage can have any relevance to deeper ideas about democracy. Initially, I couldn't see any relevance myself. And to write about it? Certainly not. Bad taste.

At first, I thought she was joking. She had been joking (often at my expense) for the past 26 years. So I began to smile when she suddenly said, in a very cold and hard voice: "I can never love you."

This was in 1982/3. The exact date, as with so many dates in that chaotic time, escapes me.

Facetiously, I said: "What's brought this on?"

"The fact," she said, in the same hard voice, "that I've never loved you. Never."

"Oh, dear," I brightly said, "and here's me thinking we've been getting on better than ever before! But I did think we shared what might be called a sort of love. Have I been mistaken?"

"Totally mistaken," she contemptuously said.

I considered the matter for all of three seconds and then just as facetiously said: "Is there any particular reason for saying so at this particular time?"

"There certainly is. I've fallen deeply in love with him."

"Him? Who?"

"John."

Since we knew a fair number of Johns, I naturally said: "Which one?"

Her reply: "John Manwaring Baines."

I don't think I have ever had a surprise in all my life as astonishing as this reply. We were alone in the flat and it was a Sunday. I sat down on our comfortable but historically child-battered settee. I could see she was serious.

All I could think of saying, for the moment, was: "Not Mr Pastry? Surely not?"

"His name," Angela stiffly and reprovingly said, "is John. I expect you to remember that in future. We're to be married."

At 57, Angela at this time was still so elegant and younger-looking that many people would have supposed her to be in her middle forties. At 74, Mr Baines was old enough to be my father. He had a moustache like worn-out sandpaper – plus tobacco-stained teeth and trembling hands.

Stunned but compliant (for I had no wish to stand in the way of a free choice), I said: "How soon do you want to start sorting all this out? Deciding what's what and that sort of thing?"

Here reply was crisp. "As soon as Sae is well enough to be told." (Sae was Mrs Baines.) "We have to think of Sae."

Still stunned but able to feel some curiosity, I said: "Does anyone else know of this plan?"

"Not yet. For the time being, we have to think of Sae. John, don't forget, was once a medical student. He will know the right time for telling an invalid – in a way that's as kind as possible."

"Unlike the way you've told me," I felt like saying; instead, I politely asked: "What made this the right time for telling me?"

Still in her implacably cold voice (a tone I had never before heard), she said: "I had no intention of telling you. I don't really know why I've told you about it. I shall have to ask John to forgive me. He wants our plans kept confidential. Remember that yourself, please. Don't go around blurting things out."

We didn't speak for the rest of the evening and retired to our separate rooms as if we were strangers in a small and rather seedy hotel.

Although not having recovered from the bust-up with Kathleen, I was able (in the wee small hours) to see why Kathleen had been so fascinated by Angela. I doubt that Kathleen would have liked to have known it, but Angela had the same effect upon certain people as Mrs Thatcher was said to have had. The cold, Snow-Queen tone of the dialogue I have quoted had reminded me, even if it doesn't remind anyone else, of Mrs Thatcher (insofar as I had seen her on television).

And here's the really weird thing …

Angela hated Mrs Thatcher to a degree bordering upon mania. I didn't greatly care for Mrs Thatcher myself because I didn't care for her policies. I can certainly understand how she could be personally hated by, say, the miners whom she treated so coldly. But Angela's hatred for her had no personal basis. Angela came from no Labour background. She had been bred, as it were, in the ranks of the Hastings Young Conservatives. Her major relatives in the town were all shopkeepers. Locally, she was exceptional in having "switched" to Labour and in becoming a great fan of Harold Wilson and then Tony Blair. She never actually joined the Labour party but she fully supported it – with Mrs Thatcher (almost her exact age) as the devil incarnate.

I won't now conceal the fact (which I was ignorant of for years) that Angela, like Mrs Thatcher, was already succumbing to the insidious mental disease now known as Alzheimer's. I didn't even know its name at the time of her secret "engagement" to Mr Pastry. Ordinary doctors were unversed in the subject. Dementia was still an unopened book for most of the medical profession. Even among the psychiatrists, such as Dr Karen Horney, dementia was never cited as a possible explanation for a certain form of "strange" behaviour. Meanwhile, people who acted strangely were regarded as "bonkers," "dotty," "dippy" or of course "neurotic."

Nor was it known in Literature. Even the wife of Dr Anthony Storr wrote a first-rate biography of William Thackeray (one of my heroes) without realising that his 'dippy' wife clearly had dementia. I, too, had read all the novels of Thomas Hardy (another of my heroes) and had studied his life without realising that his wife was another dementia-sufferer. All the obvious symptoms were apparent in every case, as in Angela's, but simply not observed ("quantified").

Kathleen had been the first person to tell me that "something was wrong" with Angela, but, in titteringly advising me that psycho-analysis was needed was not so intuitive. Psycho-analysis, even if it is only skin-deep, can do very little for a dementia-sufferer. As I've already revealed my efforts to persuade Angela to see a shrink were fruitless. But my own "analysis" was just as fruitless. I thought her problems to be self-hatred, as so brilliantly defined by Dr Horney, and that analysis of the hatred for Mrs Thatcher might remedy the often-strange behaviour.

May I hope not to be misunderstood at this stage of this memoir? I am not suggesting that anyone deciding upon an "age-gap" marriage is demented. Locally, I knew of six "age-gap" marriages – all of them happy. The very first "real writer" I had met (Bill Naughton) was married to a wife younger than himself and so was Fred. What was strange about Angela was that she was pursued by an elderly stalker in the early years of our marriage. She had been so terrified of him that I had to hover in wait and make a citizen's arrest. Yet here she was, without any advance notice, announcing a decision to marry a man very like the man I had to take to the police-station.

VIII

She was similarly terrified of the boy-friend from hell. (She was, incidentally, among the first to use that description which, today, is used for other applications.) I only met him once. It was a few months after a certain registry-office wedding (the one I had described to Kathleen as being as sparsely attended as a pauper's funeral).

He was a post-war follower of Sir Oswald Mosely and had bullied Angela into attending the London revival-rallies in 1947. I was but an inky schoolboy at that date, as Angela put it, she being those six years older than I. He was so extreme, she had told me, that he had been expelled from the party. She had broken with him completely. One day he appeared on the sea-front when I was walking with her. He seized her by the wrist and loudly said: "Why is it I was not told of this?" (By "this," he was indicating me, her husband, with a fierce toss of his head.)

I was a strong young man and I didn't really need the gallant assistance of a worried passer-by. Angela falsely assured this passer-by that the apparent attacker was "our friend" and that "we knew him well." This barely pacified friend then demanded that both Angela and I would have to attend a meeting, that evening, to discuss his disregarded "rights." His arrogance was grotesque, but so, it seemed to me, was Angela's response to it. Tearfully, as soon as we were home (at that date the cosy mews cottage), she began begging me to go with her to the stated meeting. My refusal reduced her to so much agony of mind that I had to agree.

He greeted us at the Queen's Hotel bar and sternly bought us drinks. After a few moments, he ordered Angela to leave so that he and I could discuss the best way to arrange his future relationship. She obeyed him, going off to the ladies' room with a meekness that would amaze anyone knowing her in later life. Her subjection was total. He then proposed that he and I should "share" the woman I had married.

"I won't be coming back to Hastings very often," he said, "but, when I do, I expect to exercise my right to see her if I so wish. It's a fair way of settling things. She will agree. After all, I've known her a lot longer than you. I'm willing to shake hands on it," and he extended his hand commandingly.

I knew nothing, at that time, of the discoveries by Dr Karen Horney and what she says about women in the grip of these forms of subjection. Nor was I to read anything of Tressell until 1962 – a good few years after this sea-front experience. I was a very young man and in no way sophisticated. I simply ignored his hand and formally requested him to leave and to molest Angela no further. He got up and walked out. I was left to await Angela's cautious return.

"No need to take any more notice of him," was all I said on the matter. It appeared to have long-term effect, but six or so years later she silently handed me a cutting from a national newspaper.

She seemed to be in one of her little trances. The cutting was an account of his conviction, in London, for beating up his wife in the street. Passers-by had to come to her aid and had testified against him. (He only avoided prison because the newly-married wife pleaded with the judge for leniency.)

I said to Angela: "Why have you shown me this?"

"I just thought you might be interested," was her strangely vague reply.

"You're not still seeing him, are you?"

"Oh, no – not at all."

"I can only say," I told her, giving her back the cutting, "that you've had a very lucky escape."

"Oh," she said, in a dreamily complacent tone, "he would never have done anything like that to me."

By the time of her declaration of love for Mr John Manwaring Baines (in 1982/3), Angela was so self-possessed and so worldly as to seem like a different woman; but, thinking of her earlier disastrous relationship, I decided to test this Baines love-story. I hardly knew Mrs Baines, but I had just once been invited to tea, with Angela, and I was remembering all too clearly the enticing aroma of her scones. I couldn't really believe that Mr Pastry (as I still saw him) would give up all that amount of domestic comfort for Angela. I have to reveal, ungallantly, that Angela was the untidiest of ladies and had no interest in housewifely talents. Mrs Baines was the opposite in every way, and, moreover, despite being elderly, didn't strike me as ailing. She seemed remarkably robust and, in fact, was to outlive her husband.

For the first time in our marriage, I knocked at Angela's door. (We had separate rooms.) This was the morning after her declaration and she had become a stranger. You can't just barge in on a stranger, can you?

Hearing no sound from within, I entered.

She astonished me afresh, this time by sitting up in her usual bright way. A complete change.

"Ah," she cried, "corpse-reviver! How very welcome …" (I had brought her a mug of tea.)

But I have to mention that at no time was she to express any regret for the Snow-Queen tone of the day before. Nor was she to show the slightest concern for any possible feelings that I might have had. Any effect upon me of her further revelations didn't interest her. Having let one cat out of the bag, she was animated only by the thought of letting out still more.

It was a little like Kathleen's manner at the end of the encounter in Bristol. But only a little. Kathleen, if you remember, had stopped short in her revelations. Angela, by contrast, was now gaily determined to tell me everything.

I was sitting on her bed, half-turned towards her with my own mug of tea. It was our customary morning conference, but this time she said: "Am I about to be psycho-analysed? Oh, goody! Greetings to you, Dr Freud. How nice of you to call so nice and early."

As always, I appreciated her wit, but I was in no mood to match it. I said: "Angela, I'm confused. When did this relationship actually start?"

"Oh," she airily said, "at about the same time as all that Tressell palaver."

This information was quite a jolt. "You mean during the filming of the mural-business? As long ago as 1970? Twelve years?"

I had been assuming, from the declaration of the day before that her affair with Baines had been of recent and acceptably discreet origin.

"More or less that time," she chattily said. "As I've told you before, he's been after me for years. I never let him get anywhere, not until all that Tressell stuff gave him a good excuse for inviting us both to go with him – on his photo-jaunts."

Slowly dawning comprehension: "All over Romney Marsh, do you mean?"

"Yeah," she drawled. (She often adopted a drawl for certain

occasions.) "Exactly. All over good old Romney Marsh. Including the time when all three of us nearly ended up in the dyke. It was soon after that when I let John have a bit of a go. He used to brush up quite well in those days, you might be surprised to hear. But David, it was so awfully funny. He was a real scream without his trousers. Still is."

Not wishing to bore anyone with too many details of elderly sexuality, I am omitting most of her satirical remarks. She ended them by saying: "I know what's in your mind, Quaker boy. You're right. John is no longer up to full hanky-panky. For me, it's not a matter of all passion spent. I just need to happily settle down. I've had all the flings I want. I was fertile you know, until past fifty. Dr Davy warned me. He always said I could conceive at the drop of a hat. That's why he put me on the same pill as Mrs Thatcher. These doctors share that sort of information. I had to accept it. So John is ideal. He's so distinguished and yet so incredibly amusing. I'm proud to have his love. I'm proud to give mine. And now for brekker!"

At first, when she had said the word 'flings,' I had thought she had said 'things.' Looking at her happy face, I was suddenly aware of all the clues to previous infidelity flooding into my mind. Today, when infidelity is almost as common an action as shaking hands, nobody would be very shocked by what I was told that morning. But I was as old-fashioned as Robert Tressell in my views on marriage. I admit to being shocked, yet a good part of the shock was the realisation of my own blindness to the clues. I'll state just one. During the very last motor-trip around the churches of Romney Marsh (for Mr Pastry to photograph them for one of his public talks), he was being especially skittish. Chortling, he said to me: "How funny it is to think that your wife only needs to change Haines to Baines if she and I were to get married! Just one capital letter is all it would take," and Angela had smiled, as I was now realising, knowingly and delightedly.

I was also realising that Angela must surely be in the throes of an unresolved inner conflict. Without wishing to denigrate an older generation, I couldn't help thinking that Angela could do a lot better for herself. She was still an attractive woman. Why on earth would she wish to marry an old man not in the best physical shape? Being as I then was a reader of Dr Horney's books, I naturally thought Angela's choice could be due to some sort of neurosis.

To put this latter point another way, it wasn't just the clues to infidelities which I had overlooked. I was also overlooking the obvious clues to dementia. But those clues, particularly in those days, were all the more insidious for not being glaringly obvious. I simply accepted them as being a part of the feminine character. The excessive purchase of shoes, for example, which she would chuck in the dustbin if she found they didn't fit as well as she had supposed. And what of the fortune she spent on coats and dresses? What of the way she would "clear them out" after not even wearing them? And then replacing them with other equally expensive garments – only to repeat the same routine? And what about the sometimes weekly visits to a top-flight hairdresser? Was that extravagant or was it normal female behaviour? Mrs Thatcher's similar visits were well-known and were surely just typically feminine?

The only positive sign of future full-blown dementia I had ignorantly noticed were Angela's "little trances" as I called them. These were so slight, to begin with, as to be easily mistaken for moments of reverie. They could, however, have serious consequences. On one such occasion she scalded herself with hot water and fainted from the shock. On another, just after we had bought a car, she very nearly caused me to lose my life (or cause me serious injury). She had dreamily beckoned me out of a concealed exit on a "fast" road at the very moment a speeding driver was passing. It was only a sixth sense, if there is one, which had prompted me not to obey the beckon. (There is nothing better for sharpening awareness, let me just say, than the knowledge that a spouse has very nearly killed you.) She had herself tried to learn to drive the car but had to give up after "forgetting" to turn the wheel at a certain corner out in the country. ("I can't sometimes seem able to keep my concentration," she had sufficient insight to admit.)

A big problem in recognising these "trances" was that she was so automatically adept at covering them up. They could be followed by seemingly long stretches of private charming lucidity, and, of course, genuinely intelligent interests. She was far more interested in politics than I, for example, and could get up and speak at meetings impressively. I would never do so. (I hereby reveal that it was to be Angela who, later, urged me to offer my services to Michael Foster MP. "You need to re-style some of this weak election-stuff," she had said, and it had been she, too, who had wanted to attend Fabian meetings at his house. I would only speak if she poked me.)

At this point in this memoir, I can imagine the enemies of Robert Tressell saying: "What has all this small-town gossip got to do with the claims made for the values of a bogus Socialist martyr?"

For his enemies' benefit as well as Tressell's genuine admirers, I shall now go a bit deeper and more significantly into the small-town gossip. The bits of dialogue I am repeating are for not only for revealing the nature of Angela's reasoning. They are for revealing the inspiration for another Tressellian value.

IX

Does this mean I'm claiming to be a dementia-expert? It does not. I am not a medical man. I am only offering the probable fact, on the basis of my experience with Angela, that dementia varies with individuality; and, if Angela is anyone to go by, in some very startling ways. But her condition was not a curable matter of "individuality gone wrong." Even in the next few hours of that revealing Sunday, I was to find that she was beyond any "normal" appeal to reason. How can this inspire a value? Let's see.

It was so obvious that Mr Pastry, for all his endearing qualities (and I'm not being sarcastic), was taking advantage of a vulnerable woman. He may well have married Angela if his wife had upped and left him, but that, as I realised with a sinking heart, was unlikely to happen. Meanwhile, Angela was to make every excuse for his long-term delay.

After breakfast that Sunday, I quietly began my "test" of his intentions by asking her: "How long has Mrs Baines been unwell?"

"Oh," replied Angela, dreamily but smiling, "I don't really know. We don't talk about it much."

"All of the past twelve years or so?"

"I don't really know. I don't see very much of her these days. John thinks it would be unseemly. That's why neither you nor I are invited to tea any more. He hates having to deceive her. So do I, of course. She's always been nice to me. That's why we all have to wait until she's well enough to be told."

As tactfully as I could, I asked: "Would you like me to see if I can be of any help?"

Her voice changed instantly. "What on earth do you mean? You keep out of it!" (She even clenched her fists for a moment.)

"Now that you've told me all about your plans," I delicately said as if to a child, "I might be able to move things on."

Angela's voice changed again, this time back to the Snow-Queen tone of the evening before.

"Move things on?" She repeated these words as if I said something disgusting. "As far as you're concerned, we only need to go on as we are."

Said as carefully as possible: "Angela, that just doesn't make sense. It's not how things are done."

"David," replied the Snow-Queen, "forget what I've told you. I've decided. I'm not going to tell John that I've been stupid enough to confide in someone like you. It would upset him. It would spoil his sense of fun. He likes to think he's no end of a dog. It keeps him spiced up to think he's got a secret girl-friend. All we have to do is to wait until Sae is well enough to be told. Just do what I want and everything will be all right."

Those were her exact words. Going back to my office-bedroom, I actually wrote them down (to brood upon in baffled solitude). This was after breakfast.

It was later that same Sunday, in the afternoon, that I attempted to broach the subject of divorce. By 1982, a do-it-yourself divorce was only £20 for an undefended suit. I thought it a reasonable and inevitable conclusion to the revelations.

I began by asking: "Was it necessary to practise quite so much duplicity? And for so many years?"

"Oh," she said, back in a good mood again, "that was just part of the fun. Like getting you off to Bristol as soon as I could – to leave the coast clear for John. But you wouldn't always play, would you? I tried to get you to go to Liverpool for the same reason. I like to mould situations. I've got jolly good at it, as a matter of fact."

"Angela," I said, "I hope you realise that I now feel free to try to find someone I can be happier with?"

She frowned. "You surely don't want to start another family, do you? You're physically eligible, I grant you. But you already have a family. Grown up, of course. But still a family. Two lovely boys."

Wistfully said: "Angela, it's just that I'm hoping for someone to be closer to. You've never liked living on a council-estate. So why don't you find somewhere you'd like better? We can divorce without fuss and go our separate ways."

Her reaction to this suggestion was a new shock to me.

"Oh my God," she cried, "I've lost you. I've lost you," and she dropped the magazine she had been reading and fell sideways on the settee.

I thought, at first, that it was a melodramatic act, but there could have been no faking that ghastly change of skin-colour and that weird clicking in her forehead. I thought she was having a heart-attack and was dying. (I've already stated, have I not, that

I'm no medical man?) Frantic, I did what I could in trying to bring her round; giving up, I made for the phone (to dial 999). As soon as I picked up the receiver, she was weakly screeching:: "Stop it. Why are you being so stupid and beastly? Put it down!"

Confused but concerned, I said: "Would you like me to ring for Baines?"

"His name is John," she agonisingly gasped, "and the answer is no. What's the matter with you? Why try to upset him as well as me? Make yourself useful for a change. Make me a cup of tea. Hurry it up."

I came back into the lounge with a mug of tea, facetiously saying: "Here we are – corpse-reviver," but she declined to accept it. She simply sat there, huddled up on the settee in a shivering and crouching position. Her skin-colour was only a bit better.

In a tone of passionate contempt, she said: "Can you even imagine what it's like to fall for a really handsome swine of a man? And to do everything to please him? And then find he has the most loathsome opinions? So nasty as to make you feel sick enough to die? Of course you can't imagine it. You're a mere babe."

She often referred to men (including her own relatives and work-colleagues) as "mere babes," together with phrases such as "boys with their toys" to describe what she considered to be their immature male preoccupations. Usually, she did so light-heartedly. She was now applying the mere-babe phrase to me very harshly. In an attempt to rally her better humour, I asked: "Is all this part and parcel of what you said about women being at the mercy of their own bodies?"

She took several moments to say: "I never said that."

"Oh, but Angela," I waggishly said, "you did. You told me to see if Kathleen agreed. When you so eagerly pushed me off to Bristol," I couldn't resist adding.

"It was Mrs Porter who said that," she snapped. "I was quoting her. But only a part of what she said. What she said in full was: 'All women are at the mercy of their own bodies and all men are at

195

the mercy of their own minds.' By that, of course, she meant their often silly and infantile minds. Like yours, for instance. Please now shut up. Stop annoying me."

Angela's first reference was obviously to the boy-friend from hell and was something she had never said before. She remained very silent for the rest of that Sunday, barely returning my "good night, Angela."

As for Mrs Porter, this reference (if you don't know), was to a famous old suffragette who, even as late as 1982, was not greatly known to the Hastings male population – including Fred Ball any myself. She had been the first-ever woman to stand as a local Parliamentary candidate in the year before Angela was born, and for Labour. There is now a plaque on the house where Angela went to tea with this lady (although not for that reason); and, even as I was writing the previous chapter of this book, I only knew the Council Offices in Breeds Place to have been named after her because I had to return my voter registration-form to that address. For some reason I'm not aware of, her married name has been relegated. Mrs Porter is now known as Muriel Matters (her unmarried name), but Angela always referred to her as Mrs Porter. To Angela, and rightly so, Mrs Porter was a heroine of womens' emancipation; but my own indifference was not entirely due to my sluggish male intellect. Angela had always seemed a little furtive in talking about her. Years ago, in the early years of our marriage, she had pointed her out to me in the town-centre, saying: "That's Mrs Porter," but had hurried on (even saying to me "don't dawdle") as if anxious to avoid either of ourselves being seen.

It's a loss that I was never introduced to Mrs Porter. Both Tressell and his daughter could have heard Mrs Porter giving a speech in Wellington Square (as Angela knew she had). I could easily have made a tape-recording of Mrs Porter and Kathleen discussing Tressell. (Mrs Porter died as late as 1969 and must herself have known of Fred's unabridged 1955 edition of the RTP.)

I still regret never having met and recorded that quietly retired courageous lady.

The reason for Angela's rather odd reticence (if certain readers will forgive more small-town gossip) was revealed in my next early-morning talk with Angela.

This was the Monday morning after that amazing Sunday of 1982/3. It was, as it happened, Angela's rotational Monday off. I took her in a mug of corpse-reviver. As on the Sunday, she promptly sat up to receive it. But not in any way as brightly as before.

I don't know if this is characteristic of all people with her type of early dementia, but, as was often the case, she continued what she had been saying about the boy-friend from hell as if no time had intervened. (Later in our lives, after she had been fully diagnosed, she could continue a conversation she had broken off months and even years in the past. Whether or not she did this earlier on and in her private relationship with the boy-friend from hell and others I still don't know.)

"He came into the library one day and found me talking to her," Angela calmly began to say, but not without the mug of corpse-reviver trembling in her hand. "I'd been daft enough to tell him she'd taken a bit of a shine to me. I introduced him and he was polite, but he soon found out where she stood. That night he warned me not to associate with her as he called it, ever again. If I did, he said, he would call on her and tell her about me and the Oswald Mosley thing – the British Union. I couldn't bear the thought of her knowing I was involved."

"But Angela," I idiotically said, "that sounds very much like blackmail."

"No? Really? My goodness me, David, you're not nearly as stupid as John thinks. Blackmail it was."

Disregarding this sarcastic slur upon my intelligence, I said: "Did you give in to it?"

"Of course I did. I wanted him to marry me. I would have

done anything to get him to marry me. Except wear that hideous arm-band he wanted me to wear in secret. For that, he treated me like dirt."

"Why on earth did you put up with him?"

"Ask any woman," she said, "like me or even like the precious Kathleen. John's taking me out today to lunch. He will call at half-eleven – sharp. Stay in your room and don't answer the door. Leave him entirely to me. Now get out of my sight. And stay out of his sight as well."

Anyone who has the task of looking after a dementia-sufferer will, perhaps, recognise this periodic form of insulting speech. It's one of the symptoms. But I didn't know that at the time. I was left feeling as dull-minded (and as stupid) as the old punching-bag hanging in the gymnasium at Aldershot. It didn't even occur to me to ask why she had been in fear of the boy-friend after she and I were married. (I am referring to how she had hurried me on after pointing out Mrs Porter in the town-centre, probably in 1961 – after seven years of married life.) Irrationality is in itself another symptom, but it should have been obvious to me that Angela, despite saying otherwise, was still under the man's thumb for many years after the marriage. (No wonder he had walked out of the Queen's Hotel bar, insolently confident that he had no further need to argue his case! She had secretly continued the affair.)

All I was primarily conscious of was: being among that vast contingent of spouses who, in accordance with the words of age-old gossip, are always spoken of as being "the last to know."

My own obtuseness, if I may say so, is the only irrelevant aspect of the conversations I have just set down. Every other aspect will be fully relevant to my thesis. But it has to remain a biographical truth that Tressell, now that we know he was divorced and not widowed, must have suffered a feeling of betrayal which none of us (including Kathleen) had even guessed. It couldn't have been helpful to his physical state of health. And for how long he would have kept attractive women at arm's length, had he lived beyond the drafting of his manuscript, remains an uncertainty. We who are left can only discern his state of mind through his own written words. This can certainly help us to become conscious of him as having been a real human being. We can thus discern his deeper values – even the values which we can discover in matters he didn't fully treat (such as the personal and political subjection of women).

X

I must at this stage enter an important personal disclaimer. It relates to the remaining 34 years of my marriage to Angela – making 60 years in all. During that time, towards the end, she would often say (as I was putting her to bed): "You treat me like dirt. I'm going to report you to the police." But she would also say, usually in the morning: "I've done bad things. I don't know how you can endure me. Are you by any chance some sort of saint?"

I was far from being a saint. I was often not following the Somerset Maugham dictum I had mentioned to Kathleen ("The right thing to do is always the kind thing to do"). I didn't even know Angela had any form of dementia until long after she had retired. I don't think I ever understood my own feelings.

All I can put into words was the feeling of being trapped, alone, on a desert island. It was then like growing a separate limb that I neither wanted nor needed – a deformed and useless third arm, let me unkindly say. But with no anaesthetics and equipment for sawing it off. Single mothers saddled with an impossible and even an evil-minded child are just about the only people who understand this comparison. My plight wasn't as bad as that, obviously; but, until Angela retired and became fully overcome by dementia, I was always hoping I was wrong about Mr Pastry. Perhaps he would marry her?

But it was not to be, although he had given her what he called a "promissory" ring. (She had cast her wedding-ring into the sea off the pier.) Yet she had always come back from her excursions with Mr Pastry absolutely brimming over with happiness. It's one of the reasons why I have named him but have not named the boy-friend from hell. No surviving relatives of the late Mr Baines need be ashamed of a likeable but silly old chap who, whatever his faults, had brought a form of happiness into Angela's life. I see no such reason for naming the boy-friend from hell and thus embarrassing any of his surviving relatives. I had known some of them slightly. They were said to be ashamed of his beliefs and behaviour. Also, it's always possible that he changed his politics (although not his male arrogance) before he died.

But many other women I have known, including my mother and other relatives, had all suffered dire subjection by men. On the principle that all experience is of some worth (another Tressellian value?), I think it relevant to have revealed my own witness to female subjugation. Will this help men to look more deeply into the RTP and their own often self-unbeknown acts of subjugation? I can only hope so while pointing out that such acts are not necessarily sexual or even physical.

The subjugation of women is not really a separate matter from mental illness. Merely as a layman, I am astounded to find that so many women (young and old) suffer dire subjugation as well as mental illness and mental disease. (There is a big difference between those two terms. Mental illness is curable; mental disease, on the whole, is not.)

Can I therefore also hope (even if it was unnecessary for the better-informed) that I have helped to make it clearer that dotty, potty and "crazy" people are more complex than many "normal" people suppose? And that complex needs require complex treatment? It's also an incidental but vital matter that mental illness and disease, although not infectious, can be extremely damaging to "normal" family –members who bear the main brunt. (Among writers more modern than Thackeray and Hardy who had undiagnosed wives was Raymond Chandler. His wife had a separate disease which disguised her dementia. Readers interested in literary matters should read his published letters.)

What makes my own account of Angela's dementia relevant to this memoir?

I am not in any way discounting the importance of any form of mental ill-health in the male. But the relevance of the account illustrates the point, I hope, that subjugation and mental ill-health in women is an existing menace to Western civilisation. As Karen Horney reveals to us, it is still thought "normal" in Western society to suppress the inner human growth of women.

Yes, yes, I do know that a lot of women can be as silly and as stupid as men and just as evil as men. But I think it a safe bet that we would have fewer wars and less violence if genuinely unsubjugated women were to "balance" every aspect of human life. At the moment, most men don't know that their "natural" subjection of women damages their own mental well-being.

And that of the children.

But perhaps I'm wrong. Perhaps it is "perfectly natural" for people to want a daily diet of violence and murder on their television-sets. I once counted up the number of fictitious murders depicted on a day's television and I was astounded. It was impossible to count up the even greater number of characters physically attacked. To sock people under the jaw is now ritualistic on television for teaching men how to be "real" men. And, of course, it might always have to be "natural" to prosecute a mentally-sick woman for stealing a small tin of fish in real life.

And, of course, "perfectly normal" to prosecute someone for calling someone else a tinker.

So I do hesitate to make the following practical suggestion. It might result in more people being prosecuted for using words like "daft," "dippy," "potty," "dotty," "crackers" – and, of course, "crazy." It is, I would agree, desirable to discourage ignorant people from calling evil-doers "demented." Dementia is not in itself a symptom

201

of evil. But political–correctness at its most ludicrous can only itself be a symptom of an entire nation "gone barmy."

Now that I've uttered another of the words that might one day get me arrested, I can only hope that other people have already thought of the same suggestion I am about to make. (Surely it's nicer to share the same future cell with like-minded people?)

It was the RTP and similar books which inspired the necessity, having depicted the physical effects of poverty, of a free National Health Service.

Mental health, as I was to find in looking after Angela (as well as in private discussions with other spousal-carers) was (and still is) regarded as something of a side-show. Without going into too much detail, I have to say that it was often an absurd side-show. For Angela, the help was actually damaging when I first sought NHS help in 1999 for treatment of her "weirdness." She was prescribed pills which reduced her ability to communicate (even by gesture) to zero. As for the residential care I later selected for her (not in fact free), it belonged to the horrific era of Charles Dickens. It had been portrayed to me as being "like a holiday-camp," a portrayal which was simply a falsehood. As you might expect of Angela of the Upper Fifth, she escaped after two days. She didn't actually clamber down a drain-pipe but somehow got out after somehow phoning for a taxi. She couldn't remember our home-address, but the exhausted driver managed to find it after some two hours (instead of ten minutes).

I am therefore suggesting (wouldn't anyone?) that we need a related but separate National Mental-Health Service. It will need to be separately funded, separately housed and separately managed – with its own research-and-training departments. Equally importantly, it will need to incorporate all those marvellous voluntary organisations that help family-carers (specific to mental-health disorders).

For trying to achieve a well-balanced nation, isn't this a better idea than relying on the chaos of an indistinct side-show? Wouldn't it also help to eradicate the welfare racketeers?

Of course it's a better idea!

Unfortunately, there is a drawback. It's a pity that it has to be mentioned, but tyranny is always lurking off-stage. The very fact that many psychiatrists are already relying upon pills as a form of "short therapy" is something of a horrible warning. It would be all too easy for state-psychiatry to become the arm of a vanquished democracy. Dr Horney warned a long time ago of the dangers of short therapies, but I doubt if she knew they would today be excluding any form of personal counselling – let alone psycho-analysis.

Merely as a layman, I have lost count of the number of people who, in mentioning their mental-health problems, have been told their problem is "too complicated" to treat. It's pills or nothing. Individuality has to be sacrificed to a routine formula. The justification, of course, is that there are "simply not enough" psychiatrists to treat the increasingly pandemic number of patients.

In addressing that justification and suggesting an expedient, may I say (if it hasn't been apparent) that I am an awed admirer of the medical profession. But in no way do I have the talent and courage to be a member of it. In particular, I shrink at the thought of being a shrink. From books and lectures, I have learnt to recognise a psychopath when I meet one. To me, ever since, the psychiatrists who have to cope with psychopaths are heroes and heroines of a very high order. And that's only one of their jobs.

It therefore pains me to say that doctors of all kinds often don't seem to have ordinary commonsense. I am old enough to remember how stupidly many doctors opposed the formation of a national health-service. I can remember a doctor fist-thumping a tea-table. He even frightened all the tea-things, making them jump up and down. Today, doctors can behave in the same stubbornly daft way about mental health.

How can it be anything other than daft, for example, to send a Russian psychiatric nurse to "evaluate" a "crazy" Hastings patient? I am supposed to be normal, but I was unable to understand this very young nurse myself. She couldn't speak one word of English correctly. I had to get her to write the questions which she was trying to ask Angela. And what did I then discover? The questions were in no way appropriate to Angela's life and interests.

Wouldn't it have been far more efficient to have sent a trained volunteer who had local knowledge? The questions, and indeed the little manual exercises, were so banal and routine as to be virtually useless. They hardly required psychiatric training to administer. I did complain (tactfully, I hope), but received no reply. (Possibly my linguistic objection was dismissed as racist.)

Another of my grievances: it was to be two or three years, after this evaluation, before I was able to persuade a doctor of that time to impart a diagnosis. This, alas, was no longer the era of the helpfully indiscreet Dr Davy. Even the nicest of doctors were now in terror of their own hindbound code of political correctness. We were by this time living in Sheltered Accommodation to facilitate Angela. Yet I, as her primary carer, was not a allowed to know what was "mentally" wrong with her. I had to insist, outside the door as the doctor hurried off, that I needed to know in order to know how best to treat her. As if conveying a military secret in the lurking presence of the Gestapo, he was good enough to whisper the truth about her mental state. I am not endangering his career by revealing his indiscretion because he has long been retired. All I had been allowed to know was that she had osteoporosis – an additional but physical ailment. This had long been obvious to everyone and was the "official" reason for our move into smaller but comfortable Sheltered Housing. Insidiously, it "masked" the dementia for a long time.

XI

Today, the attitudes to dementia are more enlightened, but there is still a long way to go even in medical circles. I must frankly tell you that I gained more advice from a private meeting of "primary carers" in a room over that Pub in Robertson Street than I did from the doctors. They didn't really swing into action until Angela was dying (in 2014). No psychiatrist ever attended her.

This brings me to the constructive suggestion for relieving the "shortage" of psychiatrists. Even with a fully-established mental-health service, the shortage will always be a problem if it's ignored.

In simplifying my suggestion, I am only trying to make it understandable in as little space as possible in this chapter. But wouldn't it always be an advantage to mental-health treatment to enlist the aid of each local community?

To repeat what I said earlier, anyone who can understand the RTP is perfectly capable of understanding the wisdom which talented psychiatrists have always been willing to share with the public. I am NOT suggesting that these readers should be encouraged to conduct an in-depth analysis. This memoir warns against lay attempts at such a risky task. Analysis as a form of psychotherapy is a task for a psychiatrist alone and for this reason: he or she is, or should be, a qualified medical doctor as well as a psychologist. Reactions to analysis can be alarmingly and medically physical. Only a medical doctor is legally and professionally qualified to deal with them. That much said (which shouldn't need to be said), it remains a truth that many volunteers are capable of helping out with the simple preliminaries which take up so much of the analyst's time.

Yes, these volunteers need training and need to be wisely selected; but even a reading of a simple volume, such as the short book edited by Karen Horney *Are you considering Psycho-Analysis?* might well be the only academic training needed. As for selection, why should that be a problem? Among all types of medical worker, psychiatrists are supposed to be the best equipped for judging intelligence and character.

But there is another valuable source, is there not?

It is, of course, that vast pool of potential and former patients of the psychiatrist. Even I, as a non-psychiatrist, have been impressed by these stranded sufferers. They are often not only usefully articulate but concerned about the plight of other sufferers. They, it seems to me, would be highly enlistable for conducting preparatory discussion groups. Is this all that new an idea? It is not, it has to be said. The Philadelphia Association, in Hampstead in London, has been on-going since the book-writing "revolutionary" psychiatrist R.D. Laing helped to establish it. But that's in Hampstead. Also, R.D. Laing was something of a Rasputin-like figure and not everyone's preference. But he and his friends, some of them from the 1960's New Left, did pioneer the unthinkable notion of having therapists and sufferers working together. That, in the provinces, doesn't tend to happen. Locally, in suffering from a mental-health disorder, you can find yourself as isolated as a dead fish washed up on the beach after a storm. And as a carer, too.

I can speak from personal experience on that last point. In looking after Angela, I would not have survived had it not been for voluntary local organisations like Care for the Carers and the Association of Carers. Looking after her, although I had help, did become a bit despairing. But I didn't feel real despair until I was sorting out her chaotic bedroom too soon after she had died. Thomas Hardy, the novelist I have mentioned, found a document in similar circumstances. It was written by his wife and entitled *What I think of my husband.* Wisely, he destroyed it and said no more. I, on the other hand, found no such document. But I did find copious old diaries. They were not flattering. Some receipted bills and other scraps also left me reeling with shock. I thought I'd "gone mad" myself. I had to make a round of some previous friends and close acquaintances to confirm my facts. One married couple had never noticed any sign of dementia whatsoever or even any sign of "romantic" behaviour. Most other people knew parts of the truth. One was able to tell me more than I knew myself. Another said: "Well David, I did try to drop a hint. I couldn't say more at the time. I had a boastful husband

I was stupidly trying to keep. You, David, have been a fool. But who am I to talk? Join the club."

Just one lady didn't altogether surprise me by calling me a liar and saying: "You treated her like dirt. She told me so. All you did was to loll about at home while she earned the money you spent on your hobbies. You ruined the life of a good friend of mine and you're now blackening her name."

Strangely, those last remarks helped to restore my sense of normality. It was after this emotional "straw-poll" that I began to form the thesis I'm now propounding. I also remembered more clearly what Angela had said in one of her lucid moments (about writing up "all that Tressell stuff"). After I had objected because of the matter being "too personal," she had added words I've not yet mentioned.

"Make it as personal as you can, warts and all. Including MY warts. I regret nothing."

Those last three words she spoke in French, quoting from the Edith Piaf song. (" And you can jolly well play that song at my funeral if I die before you!").

XII

Having now included a fair number of her warts in this book, as well as some of my own, I must mention something else about one of Angela's lucid moments. It was weird. The whole phenomenon of dementia is weird, but this was to be an unexpectedly weird demonstration of feminine assertion. I hesitate to call it a moment of crowning glory. That, for some tender-hearted people, might be thought too cruel a way of finally disposing of the boy-friend from hell. I'm inclined to think Kathleen would have applauded it. (I won't be saying why. I think it obvious.)

You need to understand that it was at the turn of the century when we moved into Sheltered Housing. We had a small but cosy and peaceful flat in a block humanely run by the philanthropist

James Butcher. Angela seemed to be getting better. The ghastly effects of that initial drug had worn off. Had it not been for her separate condition (osteoporosis), her remaining life would have been free from pain. As it was, she had lost 12 inches in height and was unsteady. But she began to have what I called "moments of hope" – in other words, moments of lucidity. They were just a few seconds, to begin with; then, between the bouts of confusion, they expanded into periods of lucidity, sometimes lasting for quite a time. Plenty of fresh air and exercise seemed to bring this about. She began to join her oldest chums in pub-lunches and the like. She even slowly began to compile a book for publication, encouraged by our son during his visits from Spain. (It was about her great-grandfather's military service in the Crimea.) I must say I really did think she was overcoming the dementia. But please don't assume that I condemn drug-therapy on principle. One bright day, a wonder-drug might be discovered which can expand such moments of lucidity instead of shrivelling them up.

One day the phone rang.

I can tell you the exact date because Angela noted it in her pocket-sized diary and in firmly legible writing, but I'll only give the year: 2004.

We were alone in the flat. Angela was in one of her deepest trances of dreamy confusion. She was smiling to herself in her armchair. I was at the table, using the computer. Normally, if the phone rang at my elbow, she would take not the slightest notice if she were in one of her trances.

This time, she sat bolt upright even before I picked up the receiver. She was 79 years of age. Feminine intuition, it would seem, can survive old age as well as dementia.

For a split-second, I thought it was the boy-friend from hell who was calling. Knowing a bit about the human voice (having had a dotty mother but who had taught elocution), I recognised his family tone. It was, however, his oldest and very elderly brother who was speaking.

He announced his name. Using her real name, he also announced his wish to speak to Angela.

I had never met or spoken to him before, but Angela had occasionally referred to him as being "a much nicer man" than the boy-friend. I can only say his tone had the same effrontery in it as the tone I had heard all those years ago in the Queen's Hotel bar. This was a brother who had connived at the continuing relationship by supplying the use of a flat near the library for the assignations.

I didn't need to tell Angela who was calling. From her chair, she was already snapping her fingers for the receiver. I handed it over. She was hard of hearing and the phone was therefore amplified. I heard every word. The boy-friend had returned to Hastings to die. He wanted to see Angela "for one last time." The last time he had seen her had been a long time ago but he still had a right.

I am not going to reveal what Angela said in turning down this summons. Her reply was brief and very much to the point. I can only describe her as being in a state of amazing rejuvenation. She then handed the receiver back to me. I replaced it. Congreve was dead right in his only tragedy, wasn't he? ("Nor hell a fury like a woman scorned.") Hmm. But Angela wasn't in any way furious. She was as calm and as happy as a plaster shepherdess.

Mildly, I said: "Why couldn't you have simply told him you weren't well enough to see his brother?"

It would have been the truth. She was having to overcome pain in walking and had to use a walk-trundler. She also had a bit of a cold.

"Oh but David," she said, "that would not have given me anything like the same sweet pleasure. You don't know how long I've waited for a moment as good as this. The swine now knows exactly what it's like to be totally rejected."

We discussed the call no further and she seemed to forget it within minutes, but, after she died ten years later, I found she had written in her diary the off-hand words: "Chesty cold coming and going. Phone call from" (name omitted) "re his brother. I don't want to be involved - & shan't be."

You will not understand the relevance of this act of vengeance (relevance to both Tressell and his daughter) until you have understood at least the fundamentals of Karen Horney's discoveries. Please note. I'm not saying that everyone needs to study Karen Horney's books in detail. That's never going to be possible if only for practical reasons.

But here are the two things you need to know, put as briefly and as simply as possible. And not just for understanding the behaviour of just one woman in a provincial town on the South Coast. Any hope of a truly helpful mental-health service is never going to be possible if the nature of neurotic disorder is only vaguely appreciated – to say nothing of dementia. No matter whether Karen Horney is to believed or not (as a "school" of psychology), the fact remains that her discoveries (like those of other helpful psychiatrists) are increasingly being unheeded. Short and superficial therapies are becoming the norm. Analysis is becoming politically incorrect.

The first fundamental: Karen Horney discovered that neurotic disorders are a hugely tragic waste of human energy and creativity. (An enormous amount of ingenuity goes into the making of a neurosis as a way of hiding from reality.)

The second fundamental: that different forms of neurosis are a counterfeit version of true and authentic human growth (growth, that is, into a real individual and not an artificial one).

But what is a neurosis? There are different definitions by different psychiatrists. But Karen Horney's definition is fairly easy to understand.

It is a disturbance, she tells us, in our relationships with other people. Simple as that definition is, the "disturbances" can be very hard for a psychiatrist to sort out – or for we ourselves if we try a bit of Horneyian self-analysis.

Although I warned, earlier, of the dangers of any lay person undertaking analysis, there is certainly no harm in acquainting people (as I am now doing) with certain principles of analysis. It is safe enough, for example, to point out all the principles relating to a phobia. But getting down to the reasons for that phobia is the danger-area. We don't stray into it. Why? Because Karen Horney, in her later books, added something more complicated to her definition of a neurosis.

A neurosis, she later tells us, is also a disturbance in our relationship to our very own real and authentic inner self. In other words, this being the case, the lay analyst can be straying into an area as dangerous as a mine-field. This is the area she defines as the Central Inner Conflict. Lay persons should back off at any sign of it. Anyone with a serious conflict in that area of their mind needs professional help. That being said, there does remain a lot we can learn from Horneyian psychological theory. Again, putting it simply, we can learn enough from Karen Horney to avoid suffering our own development of a central inner conflict. To put it even more simply, our little bit of self-analysis (from *Our Inner Conflicts*) is probably all the analysis we shall ever need.

And at least we will have learnt to understand why short and superficial therapies are not best practice for safeguarding true mental health. Drugs are often the only solution for psychotic conditions. We have to accept that. But for all conditions? We don't need to be psychiatrists ourselves to know that can't be right.

All the analysis we shall ever need?

Did I really say that a few moments ago? I did, yes. And I stand by it. But I am assuming that you are among the normal people who (forgive me!) are only a bit daft now and again. A vital sign of your balance will be your ability to understand Karen Horney's book *Our Inner Conflicts* almost instantly. You will find it so benign and so free from dogmatic enforcement that your individuality will feel protected right from the start. That, I'm sorry to say, is not true for other people. For one reason or another, they cannot understand even the first page of *Our Inner Conflicts*. I am not referring only to "uneducated" or "sub-literate" people but "middle-class" people of the sort we meet every day. For some, the very fact that the author is a woman is a major stumbling-block; for others, Freud still commands strict loyalty (and not just from men).

For those readers for whom even these pages are unacceptable or even beyond comprehension, I can only plead that no psychiatrist is ever immune to satire and criticism. Personally, I greatly enjoy all those films about psychiatrists who are more dotty than their patients. (I commend such films, listed in Halliwell's *Filmgoers' Companion*, as a possible antidote to too much reverence.)

Should you be more intellectual than I (and I'm not being satirical), you will find *The Self as Agent* by John Macmurray (1957) to be a further and deeper guide to the nature of the real self. But it's a far tougher book to read than his *Reason and Emotion* (1935). I had to give up. Even so, it is a regret, for me, that I never met this man who had so influenced Karen Horney. I was actually in the village of Jordans, in Buckinghamshire, when he and his wife were living there. (They had joined the Society of Friends during retirement and attended the famous Quaker meeting-house at Jordans.) I was at the time studying *Reason and Emotion* and before I discovered Karen Horney's books. John Macmurray died in 1976 after returning to Scotland. I like to think I would have become a more profound thinker if I had exchanged a few words, but I'm inclined to think not. For those mortals on the same intellectual level as I, it is the writing of Karen Horney which I recommend as more humanely systematic and understandable.

A reservation I have to make is not critical of John Macmurray. It is simply an obvious observation, but an important one for those of us researching Tressellian values.

Helpful and stimulating as his book *Reason and Emotion* is, John Macmurray states clearly that he regards Christianity as the one true religion and superior to all others. This is not a problem for Christians, obviously; but what of the Indian doctor with whom I had one of the most delightful conversations of my life? (I was in hospital and recovering from a heart attack.) She instantly understood the ideas of Karen Horney and the source of their inspiration. Should I have said: "Oh, but of course all this stuff is only applicable to Christians" and ended the conversation?

It would be rather like that schoolteacher of mine, way back in 1944, calling out "Murderers in uniform!" at those American soldiers.

I prefer to hope that future Tressellians would never make religion an unbridgeable gulf any more than they would make an unbridgeable gulf between pacifists and the military.

Ironically, towards the end of her life, Karen Horney went to Japan to extend her knowledge of Zen Buddhism. It was all part of her healing-quest. Yet the CIA tried to prevent her departure on the grounds that this pro-democracy psychiatrist might "corrupt" Japan's emerging democracy.

A bit daft of the CIA, don't you think?

XII

The whole of this Part Two is an epilogue (Part One being the prologue), but I want to end my memoir with an extra-special epilogue.

It's a return to the Tressell father-and-daughter relationship.

In my own case, I am only able to interpret it through Karen Horney and the effect upon my life by all the people involved. I am hoping that new readers of Tressell's novel will be able to interpret it in their own way and through their own family circumstances. I can see no better method, frankly, for developing a feeling for true Tressellian values – elusive as "truth" often is.

As I've said before, Fred Ball's second biography of Tressell is one of the great biographies. I cannot re-read it, myself, without remembering Fred in all his magnificently absurd bias and his clumsy concern for the man he loved. You may be surprised to hear that I re-read it with joy. But not without some rueful chortles. A broken friendship is as much a bereavement as any other.

And that goes for my broken friendship with the late Kathleen.

Why did she take refuge, as it were, in the legend she so despised? I can offer a theoretical explanation and that's all. Before I do so, let's just look at what she said in a statement she prepared for "the Meeja" in 1973 (the date of the biography). She read it out to me over the phone and I wrote it down, but, to my annoyance, I have lost one page. I don't know if she read it to anyone else or if it exists anywhere else. As far as I know, she never submitted it to the Meeja.

Sadly, although the statement Kathleen dictated to me is in my own handwriting, I have the same unresolved legal problem as I have with her letters. Until that problem is resolved, I am prevented from publishing her statement as it stands. I can only report upon it in my own words. I have the greatest respect for the Copyright laws, having myself been blatantly infringed over the years; but bad experiences with agents who seemed to think our drama-recording group was a massive film-company like MGM have made me very wary. I have been unable to trace the owner of Kathleen's copyrights. It could be a person or a firm perfectly happy with publication. But one can't assume that. All I can say is that Kathleen makes it absolutely clear that her domestic life was comfortable but not luxurious and that she and her father suffered no privations of the kind suffered by the fictitious Frank Owen. But for those of us interested in her character, the way she expressed herself (both in the text and the way she dictated it) were revealing. I'm not speaking of anything dramatic here but of the more subtle clues.

Up to a point, Kathleen had been enunciating in what Angela called her sweetie-sweet voice. She had even been a lot more complimentary than she had been previously (about the biography). But, suddenly, she began to spit balls of fire. I had difficulty in making out what more she was saying.

"To begin with," she incoherently gabbled, "as Fred does in his biography Tressell did NOT die in the workhouse!"

You will remember, perhaps, that Kathleen had dwelt upon this same point when I visited her in Bristol in 1980. It was much more of a sore point on this prior occasion. Unnerved, I dropped my Biro and was in no position to take further dictation verbatim. I had to do my best to calm her down and write the rest afterwards. She did manage to resume more calmly, but it was all disjointed. I think it best to summarise what she said about the Royal Liverpool Infirmary (as it was known as in 1911). The name had been changed. It had, it seemed, been previously known as the Royal Liverpool United Hospital. Or was it the other way round?

You have my sympathy if this is not clear to you, but, on this occasion in 1973, Kathleen quoted the official letter she had received on this vexing subject.

"Although a number of the bigger hospitals in the Liverpool area were originally workhouses, the Royal Liverpool United was not."

Having quoted this, Kathleen said in a sergeant-major type voice: "Have you got that quite clear? About the Liverpool hospitals?"

"Very clear," I hastily and falsely said.

To me, the distinction was just a split hair; to Kathleen, as I realise today, my failure to share her fury was the first of the seeds of our later discord. I think she knew and would always know I was on her side, but I was not being furious enough with Fred.

And, of course, I had Fred on the other hand blaming me for not sharing *his* fury. His Tressell had died in a workhouse and in 1980 I would be openly denying it in public. I was not just pig-in-the-middle. I was a disloyal pig-in-the-middle. And I was to run true to form, of course, by declining to write a rival biography.

This can be expressed as an axiom, can it not? In other words, those who do not share the fury of their friends cannot be their friends.

Is that an axiom Tressell would have accepted? I merely wonder. But I'm referring to Kathleen's possible unknown statement more for its sub-text than for my personal reaction to her fury.

One characteristic she certainly had in common with Angela was intuition. Not all women have it, I know; but, although scoffed at by many men, feminine intuition is, in my experience, uncannily frequent.

"Rather far-fetched," some men among Tressell's admirers might say, but I'm wondering if the word "divorce" in Kathleen's statement was intuitive. Did some part of her deeper mind know the truth about her mother? The very word "divorce" was not, even by the 1970s, a "nice" word to use. It was a word I avoided myself, as did many of my generation. So why did she say her father's domestic life was "entirely divorced" from his working-life? Why not say "entirely separate" from it?

It's also interesting (to anyone interested in human nature) that she conceded the "working part" of her father's life to be autobiographical (in full agreement with Fred's opinion). Yet, even before composing this statement, she had been telling me that he had got a lot of things wrong about Tressell's work. This disagreement with Fred over almost everything came to a head, as I have already detailed, in my Bristol encounter.

What was it that made her hesitate to issue this early statement to the Meeja? Or did she, perhaps, reveal it to any of the many visitors she received in her last years? I've no way of knowing. She and I completely lost touch in her last years. Also, all the major enthusiasts who knew Kathleen and whom I knew are either dead or in some cases are as disapprovingly out of touch as "the Tressells" became.

This means, therefore, that the reasons I suggest for Kathleen's inexplicable rejection of me are not just theoretical. They are privately theoretical. And I did not, I hasten to add, set out to "psycho-analyse" Kathleen in Bristol. I have resurrected those delicate conversations as best I can (with both Kathleen and

216

Angela) to demonstrate what might be called "accidental" analysis. (Or perhaps the better word would be "inadvertent"?) With both ladies, I found myself asking questions which, more properly, should have been asked only by a psychiatrist. Frankly, this is something which can easily happen even if you are only setting out to chat about Horneyian principles.

What's it like to find yourself "inadvertently" becoming a psycho-analyst? Allow me to tell you.

The experience won't necessarily result in coping with a fit or in your being smacked across the mouth. Quite often a simple question you might find yourself asking will result in an excessive compliment. I once asked a troubled pal of mine (and a devoted admirer of Kathleen) one of these questions. Both the question and the answer it drew from him impressed him so much that he said: "David, this is incredible. God has sent you to me."

It was this compliment which was incredible – not the question nor his answer to it. I might have been gratified by this greatest of all the compliments I have received had I not known, from my studies of Karen Horney, that it would soon be retracted. Many patients, she warns us, can go on what she calls a "binge" of health when a symptom is superficially relieved. The reason for later retraction is that no neurotic problem is solved by a single interpretation. It has to be tackled from a number of different angles. That's because the symptom has, over many years, served to allay all sorts of different anxieties. The relief from it can evaporate within an hour or so, like the dew from a morning primrose. You might then find yourself being regarded with suspicion if not aversion. Any advice you give about the need to seek professional help will be ignored (sometimes sheepishly, sometimes angrily). Psycho-analyse a friend, even only slightly, and you can lose that friend. Or (of course!) a spouse.

Karen Horney's explanation is an additional argument against "short" therapies. Whether in the form of a short talk or a pill, a short therapy can be said to be harmful because it allows the core of the problem to fester. But we can hardly blame "ordinary people" for having at least an initial faith in a short therapy. Numerous films and plays have schooled us all into believing that a shrink (usually depicted as an owlishly mature old gent) is able to resolve an entire neurosis by explaining a childhood dilemma. The troubled patient, in the shape of Bette Davis or perhaps Dirk Bogarde is lo and behold INSTANTLY transformed. He or she becomes not only a normal human being but, in older movies, a highly moral one. Because Bette Davis and Mr Bogarde were very good actors, their performance is convincing. Frankly, they were propagating nonsense. But yes, I still enjoy these films. They are good for a laugh if for nothing else.

To use Tressell's description of his own book, my "accidental" analysis of his daughter was not without its humorous side. But the result of that analysis was, for me, far from being a laugh. I still ponder over her flighty inconsistencies in the odd letter and even birthday-card after Bristol.

Although I had been unaware of Karen Horney's thinking when I was in Bristol, I was aware of Freud, Jung and Adler. (I had, if you remember, turned to them in seeking to fathom Fred.) Of those three great psychiatrists, I found Adler to be the most helpful. I still had his book *Understanding Human Nature* and, even today, I still use some of his "approaches" when I'm trying to persuade troubled people to see a shrink. As it happened, I was on the right lines with Kathleen. I can at least claim that. Karen Horney, as I later found to my amazed delight, revealed that she was "closer" to Adler than to any other fellow-psychiatrist. Also (another delight!) she had been inspired by John Macmurray's book *Reason and Emotion*.

Today, therefore, I can theorise a little more wisely than I could in 1980, but, having only my documents of Kathleen, theory is still only theory. Will it ever be validated? I doubt it.

My theory is that Kathleen began to see me as being two

separate people once she recovered from the ecstasy of confessing. One person was the "nice" boy who wrote her "nice" letters of the kind her young husband had written before they were married. (She was in Hastings; he was in London; they had written to each other every day and she had taken her stack of letters with her to Canada. She had burnt them in Canada.)

The other person she saw in me was the older fellow who had tricked her into saying more than she intended. She couldn't bear the sight of me (certainly if that angry look when I last saw her is anything to go by). But why would she have wanted to withdraw what she had said? Could it be that she had remembered more than she had said? And that she was anxious to keep it dark? On this latter point, it could of course be only the vaguest of intuitive knowledge. Possibly about Liverpool?

Yes, it's only speculative and perhaps futile to pursue. But the fact remains that her retraction prevented me from asking her even the most harmless but interesting extra questions about her father.

One particular question has begun to haunt me in these later years. I've no idea why. It haunts me every single time I visit the museum and clap eyes on the wonderful model of Lord Brassey's famous yacht *The Sunbeam*. Did Tressell ever visit this yacht when it lay at anchor off Hastings on "open-ship" days? I like to imagine he did, going with Kathleen in the passenger-boat manned by Captain Clark. I once made a tape-recording of Angela in conversation with this then very old gentleman (he was aged 107). Had he, I now wonder, ever set eyes on Tressell and Kathleen as they set out from the pier? Angela herself loved that model and had a small copy made by a model-maker. I would sometimes show it to her, in her chair, but increasingly, it meant nothing to her.

It has diminished Tressell's reality, as a person, that so many questions were never asked.

XIV

I don't want Fred's ghost wrathfully breathing down my neck as I finish this memoir. But I have to risk it. I really do have to make the following heretical statement.

Tressell's novel *The Ragged Trousered Philanthropists* was not the only novel which helped to elect the most genuine of Labour governments in 1945.

With many other Tressell admirers, Fred tended to ignore all the other British novels which had helped to bring about this ultimate change of changes. For example, even Disraeli's *Sybil or the Two Nations* (1845) had been a help. Nor would Fred even accept that *Love on the Dole* had more influence in the north of England, in 1945, than the southerly RTP.

But all these other novels didn't match the one quality of the RTP which Fred, for all his love for Tressell, had never fully appreciated.

Essentially, the RTP was analytical.

And not only that – it was brilliantly analytical. All those other novels tell us a story and leave it to us to deduce the remedies. Both Dickens and Gissing did the same. It was only Tressell who gives us characters who bear out the remedies suggested (often so fruitlessly) by Frank Owen and the token-toff Barrington. I'm not saying this made it a superior novel. I'm simply saying it made it a novel with a different purpose. That purpose (if I may repeat the word) was analytical.

Are you already beginning to guess the full heresy I am about to propound?

In describing her father, Kathleen certainly never used the word "analytical." She described him as "methodical," but this word, I suggest, is a near-enough relation. He analytically devised characters (or "methodically" devised them) to illustrate his thesis. But they are almost all suitable, as candidates, for the form of analysis known as psycho-analysis. All his main characters and even some of the lesser (such as Councillor Weakling) are to be found among the "types" described in Karen Horney's *Neurosis and Human Growth*.

Yes, what I am saying is that Tressell, had he lived longer, would have taken an even deeper interest in the subject of psycho-analysis than his daughter. It's a subject almost built for a man of his analytical talent. Given the breadth of his mind, the subject could have become the foundation for books of the kind we call great. Such speculation is futile, I agree. But I'm still hoping it's a stimulating fact that his one great novel is a treasure-house for Horneyian analysis.

So far, I've not felt any supernatural breath on the back of my neck. Perhaps I will now do so. I am about to question the word "great."

Tressell's novel is a great novel. But not in the sense that *Vanity Fair, Jude the Obscure, A Tale of Two Cities* or even *The Wind in the Willows* or the unfinished novel *Weir of Hermiston* are great.

Even when adapted for the stage, the RTP is in no way "great" in the sense that plays such as *The Heiress* or *The Master-Builder* are great.

I'm sorry to say that I did once try to discuss all this with Fred. He went so puce with rage that I had to desist. The truth is that he wasn't all that interested in drama. Neither Mr Ibsen nor Mr Shakespeare ever entered our conversation.

In novels, drama refers to the quality needed if the story is to grip all our senses. That means the novel must have what authors call a plot – a structure with a beginning, a middle and an end. Certain novels and short stories (usually referred to as "literary" fiction) don't have very strong plots. They rely on their style to keep the reader captivated. The short stories by the New Yorker writer Jean Stafford are of this brilliant sort. Her first collection *Children are Bored on Sunday* was published by Gollancz in 1954 and was the first "new" book I ever bought. (I had in my then youth only ever bought secondhand-books.) I paid eight shillings and sixpence – a simply enormous sum but I simply had to have Miss Stafford's book.

Tressell was neither in her category nor the plot-drama category. His novel was in the category known as "documentary" – i.e., a contemporary chunk of reality, usually called actuality.

Had he lived long enough to write more books, I personally think they would not have been fiction of the kind I have incompletely listed. I think he would probably have been very much a hybrid writer like George Orwell (part fiction, part actuality).

Yes, it's pointless to speculate. I agree. But my categorisation of his novel has a valid point because of the controversy over the Pope Abridgement.

Oh, dear! Surely I can now expect to feel Fred's ghostly breath hot on my neck? The subject of Jessie Pope's abridgement, for Fred, is exactly equal to showing a red rag to a bull.

I won't dwell too long on his worst reaction, but it was prompted by the publication of the London Panther Edition of the full text in 1965. Mr Alan Sillitoe, a writer I admired but never met, had written an introduction to it. Had Fred ever met Mr Sillitoe? I've no idea. Mr Sillitoe was the author of *Saturday Night and Sunday Morning*, a not altogether flattering portrait of a working-class man. Mr Sillitoe was the sort of working-class writer Fred could have been but was far too self-absorbed. At first, Fred was annoyed by the Sillitoe introduction. (Why hadn't Fred himself been asked to write it?) But Mr Sillitoe had made two comments which soon mollified Fred. Worse than mollified. They were comments which stoked up Fred's obsessive resentment of Miss Jessie Pope.

Both comments have now gone into the folklore about Tressell. The first was the often misunderstood statement that the RTP had helped Labour to win the 1945 General Election. I'm sure Mr Sillitoe didn't mean to imply that the victory was entirely due to the RTP. But that was how Fred, and numerous others, interpreted the statement. And still do.

The second statement was that the abridged version "had been made to end on a note of despair suggesting that cranks who believed in Socialism could do nothing better than think of suicide." Fred seized on these words avidly. At a small gathering of my friends in the flat, he suddenly quoted the words from an unfolded bit of paper.

"I couldn't put it better myself," he proclaimed. "What right had that woman to come between a man and his work? To sabotage his art?"

Angela was unexpectedly present. (She hadn't yet lost all interest in Tressell and most of everything else which didn't interest Mr Pastry.)

"Oh but Fred," she smilingly said. "What about a man coming between a woman and her work? I don't think you've got it quite right about the work she did on the manuscript. Nor did Alan Sillitoe."

"Bloody women," Fred burstingly cried, and he stormed out of the flat.

After trying to restrain his exit, I came back into the room to find Angela saying to my startled friends: "Fred's just Fred. Take no notice.

Having myself often muttered the words "bloody women" (probably as much as women mutter the words "bloody men"), I still can't blame Fred for his behaviour. As for Mr Sillitoe, I still can't blame him for "not getting it right'" about Miss Pope's editorial intentions. Like everyone else in 1965, he was under the full weight of the public legend. He even made the mistake (although surprising in a highly professional writer) of believing the book to have been written in the "spare time" of a man living in poverty and literally starving to death. But Mr Sillitoe did mention having had the thought, after reading the abridged version, that it had not been written by a working-class man. (Mr Sillitoe uses the expression "working man" but his context makes his meaning clear.)

I think it safe to assume that Mr Sillitoe, if he had known a little more about Tressell's real life in Hastings, would not have made that biased interpretation of the climax. He would have seen what Miss Pope was trying to achieve on Tressell's behalf and which is also obvious from her letters. But let me just add what Angela said to me after our guests on that unruly day had departed. (I've only recently remembered this.)

"If it's true that the RTP helped Labour to win the election," she said, "then Fred needs to remember that it was Jessie Pope's version what done it." (Angela often used bad grammar jokingly.) "I've read both her version and the full text. She did a good job. But she was a woman, of course. That's what he really doesn't like about her version."

I remember feebly saying: "Several parts of her version could have been done better."

"Of course," Angela robustly said, "and they would have been better if she'd had the author to work with! But she hadn't, had she? All she could do was her very best for Tressell."

"But she had Kathleen to consult," I said.

"Yeah," drawled Angela, "she had innocent little Kathleen."

What was it that Miss Pope tried to achieve for Tressell? She had succeeded if book-sales are the only standard we apply; but, if we consider the letters she wrote to the publisher she was enthusiastically urging, it's obvious enough that she was also striving to serve Tressell's purpose.

But she seems to have thought that he had set out to write an epic novel in the plot-drama category. In assuming this, she was (in my view) mistaken. Tressell's then intention was actuality. Although he fictionalised actuality to a judicious extent, he wasn't trying to be another Thomas Hardy. He wanted to stay as close to actuality as possible. That is why the story of a working-class seduction lacked any of the qualities of true drama.

For that story of a wife being seduced by the lodger to become drama, it would have needed to be about the main character Frank Owen.

As it was, the seduction concerned a very minor character with other chapters interrupting it. The results of the seduction are depicted almost as an afterthought with Frank Owen coming to the rescue of the "fallen" woman. That part of the RTP I have to admit, strikes me as weakly written although sincere. I completely share Miss Pope's opinion of it.

Miss Pope, it has to be said, was not the maiden-aunt type some people seem to imagine. As a possible guide to her character and vocation, I suggest they should read George Gissing's short tale *Comrades in Arms* about two writers of the 1900 period. One of them is the lady-journalist, a Miss Childerstone, who could easily have been a portrait of Miss Jessie Pope. In editing the wife-and-lodger episode, Miss Pope was being far from squeamish. She was trying to give the book dramatic symmetry. But she probably never realised that Tressell had been recounting a real-life story which he had either heard of or had been told in confidence. Inevitably, the details about it are banal. She must have thought she was sharpening them up. But, for us, Frank Owen's moral reaction to this sadly commonplace act of adultery should obviously confirm that Frank Owen cannot be (and never was) a literal portrait of Tressell himself. Had he wanted to portray himself, he would in all integrity have had to depict that he himself, as Owen, had suffered adultery.

Kathleen, in later years, muddled everyone by hinting that Barrington (the kindly token-toff) was really her dad in disguise. But Miss Pope was being consistent in cutting out Barrington. He doesn't even have much moral standing. How can a toff have any validity if he is taking a job away from a genuine workman in need of work? Barrington, like Frank Owen, was a fictitious documentary-device which is perfectly acceptable in depicting actuality. But, even in the full text, it has to be said that Barrington is not all that acceptable. I, for one, rather feel what it must have been like for Miss Pope to edit this mass of conflicting material – and with the enigma of the well-dressed and well-educated Kathleen having spun her not a few yarns.

So why did Miss Pope edit the manuscript in such a way as to "end on a note of despair"? And even to imply that anyone believing in Socialism needs to commit suicide?

Fred carried this accusation into his biography of Tressell. After damning Miss Pope with faint praise, he tore her to shreds in so unfair a way as to be absurd. Yet it remains a fact that a lot of people still share his view. They also sternly point to her "jingoistic" poems as another nail in her disreputable coffin. They forget all about the war-fever of 1914 as much as they do the war-fever of 1982. ("We want war," people shouted outside Downing Street, just as they had in 1914.) It wasn't only the wicked Tories who supported Mrs Thatcher's Falklands War. A Socialist friend of mine and Tressell admirer astounded me by promptly supporting Mrs Thatcher as a saviour of the nation. The point I'm making here is not on the war itself but the feverish enthusiasm which seemed to grip almost everyone – just as it had in 1914. Miss Pope died in the middle of World War Two, but it would perhaps be enlightening to research her later political views.

And perhaps her religious views as well? It might give a bit more perspective to Tressell's ironic remarks about Jesus Christ (to be found in the full text in his Chapter 22 *The Phrenologist*). What Jesus Christ "really meant" when he spoke of inconvenient things like turning the other cheek was very much in the spirit of war-fever. Jesus Christ "really meant" advice like: "Turn on him with a Maxim gun; disembowel him with a bayonet or batter in his skull with the butt of a rifle."

Putting both Tressell's ironies and Miss Pope's jingoism to one side, can we now view Miss Pope's ending rather more charitably?

Her only mistake was to regard Tressell's manuscript as a plot-drama. That being so, she was only guilty of trying to make the ending more dramatic and thus more memorable.

"This is how the hero of the drama feels," she seems to have advised the publisher, "because his good words have continued to fall upon stupidly deaf ears. Tressell has shown very vividly how feckless and fickle the working-classes are. They are their own worst enemy. We have to ram this home. The ending I suggest is a warning to them."

Perhaps if Tressell had lived long enough to join the editorial discussion, he would gladly have agreed to a change of ending to make it "more dramatic." For a plot-drama, of course, this would be far more effective than the dream-like "visionary" ending of his full text.

But, charitable as I feel towards Miss Pope, I believe her ending to be a good intention but very badly handled. To kill off the hero, in the context of the novel as a plot-drama, can only result in anti-climax. Good as her abridgement is on the whole, I found after reading it that I had exactly that feeling – anti-climax.

If we are to have an abridged version for, say, a film of a stage-show, what ending should we have which more properly fulfils Miss Pope's intention?

There can only be one which Tressell himself supplied (but at an earlier point in the text).

Surely it must be one of those war-fevered attacks by the Philanthropists? On one of those Socialist vans? One of the very vans, in fact, which Angela's valiant chum Mrs Porter brought to Hastings?

An ending like that, I suggest, would pack a heck of a wallop.

XV

Of all the sections of this memoir which I have found hard to write, this last section is to be the hardest. It contains the parting words which old-fashioned authors used to call an envoy (but for some reason spelt envoi). I'm reluctant to write it because it's about the nature of love.

No subject is more misunderstood today, an era of crass psychological ignorance combined with infantile prurience.

But there are one or two matters about Kathleen and her father which, however reluctantly, I need to make (I hope) a little clearer. Their relationship can never be properly understood if notions about it being "an incest thing" are allowed to prevail.

Love is love. It's still love between people even when those people are in the shape of a father and a daughter. But sexual fear and taboo can endanger and even ruin that love. That, in essence, is what happened to Tressell. It's why he forced himself to tear himself from Kathleen and go to Liverpool. He saw in her too much a semblance to his wife. (There was hearsay evidence for this.)

And what of Kathleen's feelings?

I think I can illuminate them a little more by referring to Angela's "inexplicable" love for Mr Pastry.

Kathleen had admired Angela and was puzzled if not hurt by her failure to respond. She sensed in Angela a form of kinship. Angela had seemed to be a woman of the world of the sort Kathleen had yearned to become. Kathleen had no idea that it was she, Kathleen, who was the more "worldly" in the best sense of that word.

It's not difficult to see why Angela failed to respond to Kathleen. She was far too obsessed with matters which pleased Mr Pastry to have any time for Kathleen. Angela, in short, was in the state of mind which Karen Horney defines as Morbid Dependency.

She had also been in that state of mind when subjugated by the boy-friend from hell. Although Mr Pastry was a far more benign choice, her dependency upon Mr Pastry was not a natural or a "mature" dependency. It was still morbid. She had simply transferred the dependency from the boy-friend from hell to the "nicer" man.

Karen Horney gives in detail all the effects of this type of dependency in a woman. As I could attest, they correspond exactly with Angela's behaviour during both those relationships. Any woman in the grip of such a dependency, especially when it's with a man of the aggressive-vindictive type, needs professional help.

At the very least, she should consult Chapter 9 in *Neurosis and Human Growth*. It is entitled *The Self-Effacing Solution: the Appeal of Love*. She then might feel able to consult the subsequent chapter entitled *Morbid Dependency*, She then might need all her strength to overcome her surprise.

"The first thing to strike us," writes Karen Horney in *Morbid Dependency*, "is such a woman's total absorption in the relationship."

Morbid dependency, as Karen Horney warns us, is not confined to relationships between man and woman. But that's the relationship which is relevant here.

Was Kathleen morbidly dependent upon her father?

No, she was not.

Although she was childlike in her teens, she had only the normal filial dependency upon him. By "normal," I mean that she had all the potential for what Karen Horney calls "human growth." You will need to study Karen Horney if you need a deeper explanation. I state only the obvious. To set sail for Canada when she was still so young was a really bold thing to do. And to perform on the stage (in opposition if not defiance) to her father's wishes was even bolder. The idea that she was a shrinking violet when she popped up in the publisher's office just has to be unlikely.

It was her father who had the morbid dependency. One indication of it was in naming his daughter as the person to be notified of his death. You need to study Karen Horney for other indications, but all were a burden which could easily have become crushing. The fact that Tressell seems to have sensed this is a tribute to his love in deciding on a break. It is also a tribute to her own potential resilience that she didn't succumb too much.

"Morbid dependency," writes Karen Horney in concluding her chapter on the subject, "is one of the most complicated phenomena with which we have to deal."

I can only add that it's all the more complicated in Tressell's case because we have no way of knowing what he was really planning. The fact that he concealed so much from Kathleen does lend weight to the strong possibility that he was concealing even more. Liverpool remains an enigma. It can't be anything else and I have to finish by saying that Angela was the first to point this out.

I would not be writing this memoir at all if it hadn't been for Angela. It was she, if you remember my mentioning it, who urged me to write such a memoir. But I am not as naïve now as I was in those earlier days. I am now more fully aware that a zeal for truth, in both ladies, was not necessarily their motive. It wasn't only Kathleen who was mischievous in wanting to cause certain people acute discomfort. Angela was the same. She had wanted certain people in her local circle of acquaintances to learn how wrong they had been – both about herself and about Kathleen and "all that Tressell stuff."

Despite her dementia, Angela's individuality (her inner human growth) had struggled to emerge.

As for Kathleen, I would still acknowledge that I would never have come across Karen Horney's books if she, Kathleen, had not earnestly suggested psycho-analysis for Angela. It was an abortive suggestion because dementia, even in its early stages, prevents normal reasoning. Any insight gained in a lucid moment, even when I was able to encourage it, always evaporated.

Did Kathleen herself suffer dementia in her final years? I have no way of knowing. If she did, it would account for a lot – especially if she was beginning to suffer dementia as early in her life as Angela. I can only say that Angela, who was a great reader, would only read but a few pages of *Our Inner Conflicts* before putting it aside. And that's when she was still a highly regarded librarian and on several important local committees. She had even started an archaeological society with a friend, Mr Alan Scott, and acted as its chairman. This was a subject that had never interested her before she began doing her best to please Mr Pastry. They held their first ardent committee meetings in our flat, with me (of course!) banished to my office-bedroom.

By that time, her interest in my own pursuits had virtually ceased. She was not interested even in the most promising developments in my own career. She declined to accompany me to events which, frankly, I thought a lot more alluring than excavations of medieval cess-pits and the like. Although we had met through the drama, she never attended any of the performances of my dialogues in London and elsewhere. ("Sorry. Another time, little one.")

Why was it that I was ignoring the painfully obvious? That, too, was a question which I was only able to answer by studying Karen Horney. It's not an answer I shall reveal, but I like to think that Kathleen was the sort of woman who would have understood it if our friendship hadn't collapsed.

I think I should finish by saying that a new quality of aloofness possessed Angela in the years following her act of vengeance in 2004. She was like a woman for whom a long-awaited purpose in her life had finally been satisfied. Unfortunately, this seemed to mean a diminishing will to stay as fit as she could. She began to refuse to go outside the flat, not even into the garden on the most beautiful of summer days.

More and more, she went sweetly mad but sometimes not so sweetly. Her moments of lucidity became less and less by the year of her death in 2014. Dreamily and repeatedly, she leafed through her private copy of *Historic Hastings*, the enormous book by Mr John Manwaring Baines with its "secret" message to her inside the cover.

When she had been told of his death, she had simply smiled to herself. She was in no way sad about it. Their whole relationship had become one of genteel playfulness, rather as if both of them were Victorian children. He used to chortle indulgently at her "left-wing" views and she would chortle at his antics and his many slanderous local-government stories.

Sometimes, it would seem, a morbid dependency can be regarded as acceptable if the parties to it are both benign and there is no possibility of what Karen Horney calls "growth."

One day in her last year, in one of her short lucid moments, Angela closed Mr Pastry's big book and suddenly said: "I don't like this place. Why am I being kept here? I want to go home."

I said: "Angela, you're already at home. It's where we live."

Her reply: "I mean home with mummy and daddy."

Glibly, I said: "Oh, but they're not far away. They're only upstairs."

She just as instantly said: "Oh, are they? Oh, good," and she happily resumed leafing through Mr Pastry's book.

In another of her short lucid moments, the next day, she suddenly said: "You should turn it into a play. It would make a very good play."

She had not made any reference to drama for a long time, nor any reference to Kathleen; but I rather gloomily thought she was referring to the scene in the publisher's office which I had dramatised all those years before. I had never mentioned that aborted script to Angela. (It was the one I had foolishly named *Sold for a Mess of Pottage* and thus caused the rift with Kathleen.)

With a sigh, I said: "What part of the Tressell story do you think would make a good play?"

"No part of it at all," she said, in an amazingly bright return to her old manner. "I'm talking about that nice little story by George Whatsisname."

I was the one to be slow to comprehend. I said: "Do you mean George Gissing? Do you mean the story called *A Daughter of the Lodge*?"

"That's right," she said. "George Whatsisname. It would make a lovely little play."

Within the next few seconds, she had forgotten what she had been saying. I had to give up trying to retrieve the lucid moment. I was left to wonder why on earth I had not thought of her suggestion myself. It would surely have avoided that rift with Tressell's daughter?

Wouldn't it?

That little question apart, there is one other relevant and vital question to answer.

What is it that we can all learn from this deep exploration of the democratic values in the Tressell story? It is surely this. For most of us, there is nothing much wrong with us that a really happy marriage cannot cure. Essentially, democratic values are emotional values.

In other words, happy and mentally-fit parents will always tend to have happy and mentally-fit kids. Tressell, I suggest, would have agreed with that statement of the obvious – and Kathleen too. Her incessant tittering was of course a substitute for her life-long tears.

HERE THIS MEMOIR (AND THE MESSAGE) ENDS.

Other books by D.V. Haines

*You can obtain copies online from the Bookshop at
www.troubador.co.uk*

*But please don't forget your public library where you
can reserve a copy for a small charge. Public libraries
will all close if we neglect to use them!*

Enjoyable Motoring
A guide to freedom from accident

Are you enjoying your driving as much as you should?

This book unveils the author's 30 years of private research into the so-called "born" drivers he has met.

How are they able (so magically!) to avoid having accidents? How are they able to concentrate so enjoyably and without apparent strain whatsoever?

Essentially, the book is about the difference between motorsport and motoring and how a proper knowledge of the difference can reduce accidents and congestion on public roads. It might also amuse readers of Robert Tressell to know that Mr Haines borrowed Tressell's format (from *The Ragged Trousered Philanthropists*) to expand his thesis.

A so-called 'born' driver has been cajoled into giving a series of lectures (to incorrigible drivers). One by one, these incorrigibles get up and stalk out.

Who, if any, will be left in the audience?

Available in print or as an e-book.

The Gentleman Shopkeeper
A Mystery Novel

An over-respectable shopkeeper in an English country-town fears he will be accused of killing a wheel-clamper. Although conceived as a narrative for audio, this character-study has had good reviews as an ordinary novel.

Nancy Kline (Goodreads reviewer):
I highly recommend "The Gentleman Shopkeeper" for both its clever intrigue, original and intricate plot, and well-developed characters. And, whether intentioned or not, it produces quite a depth of psychological insight into human nature.

Brandi Welch (freelance reviewer):
At first, I wasn't sure where this was going and the main character didn't seem to know either. But what a fun read! The quirky characters, the twists in the plot, and the eccentric language all joined together for a really fun time.

Douglas Osler (reviewer):
This will keep you laughing but it is certainly not lightweight. It is a murder story in reverse. Instead of whodunit, the reader knows that from the start and the mystery is what happens next. It is very well written and the main character is typical of buffoons we all probably know.

Available in print or as an e-book.

The Society for Better Bread
and Other Scripts

These "microphone-exercises" were written for the audio magazines of the sixties and early seventies as well as for the drama-recording groups of the period.

The society for better bread has been performed on stage at various "fringe" venues, beginning with the Royal Court Theatre in 1975, but, technically, it was an experiment with theatrical stereo. Although recording on magnetic tape has long been abandoned, this was a delightful time of many pioneering experiments in drama-in-sound and is worth remembering.

Also included: the abortive play mentioned in *Tressell and the Late Kathleen* (*Sold for a Mess of Pottage*) because this was an experiment in binaural drama-in-sound (i.e., "sound-in-the-round").

Also included: some examples of Aural Mime (the telling of anecdotes and even stories through sound-effects alone) which were first published in 1967 in *Dramatape Miscellany*.

Publication-date to be announced.

The Strange Case of
James Hadley Chase

A critical biography about the often misunderstood (but highly successful) writer whose formative years were spent in Hastings (in the town of Robert Tressell). Graham Greene once wrote to him: "You are the greatest living writer walking the earth."

Other writers were not so kind.

Publication-date to be announced.